D0565527

●═ CONTINUOUS IMPROVEMENT TOOLS
VOLUME 2

A Practical Guide To
Achieve Quality Results

Richard Y. Chang

Matthew E. Niedzwiecki

Richard Chang Associates, Inc.
Publications Division
Irvine, California

CONTINUOUS IMPROVEMENT TOOLS
VOLUME 2

A Practical Guide To
Achieve Quality Results

Richard Y. Chang
Matthew E. Niedzwiecki

Library of Congress Catalog Card Number
93-77938

ISBN 1-883553-01-6 (Volume 2)
ISBN 1-883553-02-4 (Two Volume Set)

Third printing March 1995

Richard Chang Associates, Inc.
Publications Division
41 Corporate Park, Suite 230
Irvine, CA 92714
(714) 756-8096 • Fax (714) 756-0853

RICHARD CHANG ASSOCIATES

ACKNOWLEDGMENTS

About The Authors

Richard Y. Chang is President and CEO of Richard Chang Associates, Inc., a diversified organizational improvement consulting firm based in Irvine, California. He is internationally recognized for his management strategy, quality improvement, organizational development, customer satisfaction, and human resource development expertise.

Matthew E. Niedzwiecki, Manager of Quality Management at Children's Hospital Los Angeles, is an experienced training and organizational development practitioner. His extensive background and areas of expertise include total quality management, training design, process analysis, and data interpretation.

The authors would like to acknowledge the support of the entire team of professionals at Richard Chang Associates, Inc. for their contribution to the guidebook development process. In addition, special thanks are extended to the many client organizations who have helped us shape the practical ideas and proven methods shared in this guidebook.

Additional Credits

Reviewers: P. Keith Kelly, Sarah Ortlieb Fraser, Jim Greeley, and Eric Strand

Graphic Layout: Christina Slater

Cover Design: John Odam Design Associates

PREFACE

The 1990's have already presented individuals and organizations with some very difficult challenges to face and overcome. So who will have the advantage as we move toward the year 2000 and beyond?

The advantage will belong to those with a commitment to continuous learning. Whether on an individual basis or as an entire organization, one key ingredient to building a continuous learning environment is *The Practical Guidebook Collection* brought to you by the Publications Division of Richard Chang Associates, Inc.

After understanding the future *"learning needs"* expressed by our clients and other potential customers, we are pleased to publish *The Practical Guidebook Collection*. These guidebooks are designed to provide you with proven, *"real-world"* tips, tools, and techniques—on a wide range of subjects—that you can apply in the workplace and/or on a personal level immediately.

Once you've had a chance to benefit from *The Practical Guidebook Collection*, please share your feedback with us. We've included a brief *Evaluation and Feedback Form* at the end of the guidebook that you can fax to us at (714) 756-0853.

With your feedback, we can continuously improve the resources we are providing through the Publications Division of Richard Chang Associates, Inc.

Wishing you successful reading,

Richard Y. Chang
President and CEO
Richard Chang Associates, Inc.

TABLE OF CONTENTS

"Quality in a product or service is more than what you put into it, it's what your customer gets out of it that counts."

Anonymous

CHAPTER ONE

INTRODUCTION

In *Continuous Improvement Tools Volume 1*, seven popular and well-known planning, analysis, and interpretation tools (*Brainstorming, Affinity Diagram, Matrix Diagram, Force Field Diagram, Cause and Effect Diagram, Criteria Rating Form, and Check Sheet*) were introduced. In *Volume 2* we continue this process by introducing eight additional tools (*Tree Diagram, Pareto Chart, Sequence Flow Chart, Process Flow Chart, Scatter Diagram, Run Chart, Control Chart, and Histogram*) that are used during the various stages of a quality-improvement effort.

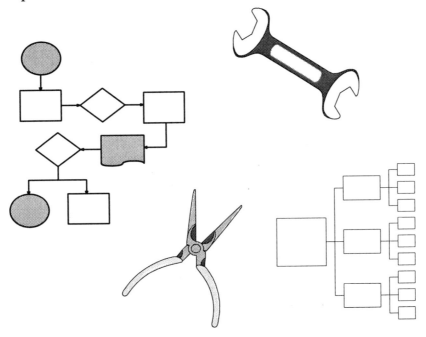

Continuous Improvement Tools Volume 1 featured an easy-to-understand reading format that combined practical examples with concise explanations. *Volume 2* builds upon this format with easy-to-use forms and checklists at the end of each chapter to help you answer the question: *"Which tool should I use and why should I use it?"*

Think of the eight tools in this volume as additions to your quality-improvement or problem-solving *"tool box."* These tools can be pulled out and used during team or individual process-improvement or problem-solving efforts.

Why Read This Guidebook?

Read this guidebook when you or your team are working on a process-improvement or problem-solving effort that is: stalled, unstructured, taking too long, in need of new ideas, or has failed in the past. In short, read this guidebook when you want to try something new to help your process-improvement or problem-solving effort succeed.

Who Should Read This Guidebook?

As with *Continuous Improvement Tools Volume 1*, the potential audience for *Volume 2* is broad. Everyone from front-line employees to executives will find it accessible, practical, and full of ideas which can be applied immediately!

When And How To Use It

This guidebook is designed as a quick and easy-to-use reference to support your process-improvement efforts. Use it during meetings, working with teams, or in your personal work area.

When deciding which tool to use, take a moment to look at the selection matrix below. Whether you need a tool for planning, analysis, or interpretation purposes, you'll find these tools useful, practical, and adaptable.

To get meetings off to a good start, have team members read in advance the chapter explaining the tool being used.

TOOL (USE)	Planning	Analysis	Interpretation	Team	Individual
VOLUME 1					
Brainstorming	✗	✗		✗	
Affinity Diagram	✗	✗		✗	
Matrix Diagram	✗			✗	✗
Force Field Diagram		✗		✗	
Cause and Effect		✗		✗	
Criteria Rating	✗		✗	✗	
Check Sheet		✗	✗		✗
VOLUME 2					
Tree Diagram	✗			✗	
Pareto Chart			✗		✗
Sequence Flow Chart	✗	✗		✗	✗
Process Flow Chart	✗	✗		✗	✗
Scatter Diagram			✗		✗
Run Chart		✗	✗		✗
Control Chart		✗	✗		✗
Histogram		✗	✗	✗	✗

TREE DIAGRAM

The Tree Diagram is a planning tool used to:

- 👉 **Map out the path and tasks that need to be accomplished in order to achieve a primary goal and all related subgoals**

- 👉 **Organize the sequence of tasks in an implementation plan**

- 👉 **Check the logic in a plan by looking for possible gaps**

Completing a Tree Diagram consists of five major steps:

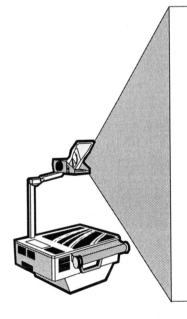

STEP 1:	Start the Tree Diagram session
STEP 2:	Brainstorm tasks
STEP 3:	Identify major tree headings
STEP 4:	Create the next level of detail
STEP 5:	Review the Tree Diagram

Frank, a computer support technician . . .

was having difficulty keeping up with the huge pile of customer messages he received daily. Messages *(voice mail and handwritten)* would pile up faster than he could return them. He assembled a team of other computer-support technicians and together they decided *(through a structured, problem-solving process)* the company's voice mail system needed to be upgraded. Management agreed to the decision *(after all, the voice mail system was ancient)* and the team now needed an implementation plan. Frank wanted to try using the Tree Diagram because he had read it was a good tool to help create an implementation plan. . . .

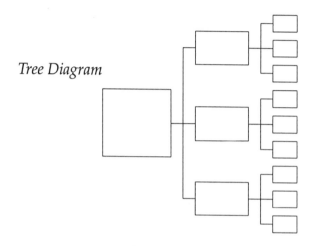

Tree Diagram

Step 1: Start The Tree Diagram Session

➡ Set a time limit for the session. Generally, 45-60 minutes is sufficient.

Note: Plan on taking more than one session to complete the Tree Diagram.

➡ Select someone in the group to be the Recorder. The job of the Recorder is to write potential tasks or process steps on a flip chart, sticky notes, or 3" x 5" cards.

➡ Identify your goal. In your team or work group, agree on a simple statement describing the corrective action or problem solution to be implemented. Write this statement in the box on the left side of the diagram.

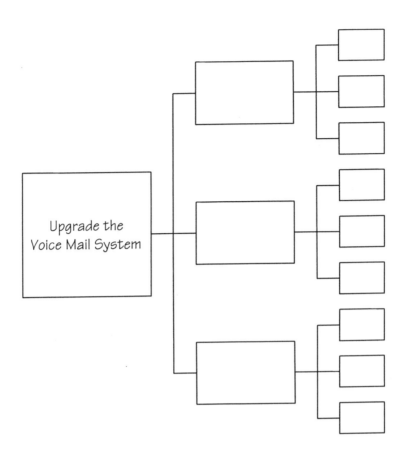

Diagram # 1 - State your goal

Frank had called a 2 *P.M.* meeting . . .

specifically for implementation planning. It was now 2:01 P.M. and everyone on the team was present. Frank reviewed the Tree Diagram he had sketched on a flip chart, and then asked for a volunteer to be the Recorder for the session. Penny stepped up to the three large sheets of flip chart paper taped to the wall and stood ready to record. The group members had no trouble identifying their goal—upgrade the voice mail system. Penny wrote this in the box on the left side of the Tree Diagram *(see Diagram # 1)*. . . .

Step 2: Brainstorm Tasks

Your job now is to brainstorm all the steps or tasks that need to be accomplished to reach the identified goal.

Frank told the group . . .

the next step was to brainstorm tasks they'd have to complete before reaching their goal. As the group brainstormed, Frank asked the question: *"What tasks must we complete in order to implement the new voice mail system?"* As the team offered their ideas, Penny wrote them on sticky notes and placed them randomly on the flip chart paper. After 20 minutes, the group agreed they had generated enough tasks to begin the next step *(see Diagram # 2). . . .*

Diagram # 2 - Brainstorming tasks

Step 3: Identify Major Tree Headings

When you have completed the initial brainstorming *(this could take the entire 45-60 minutes)*, choose the tasks you consider the most important *(e.g., researching the cost, hiring new employees, choosing a vendor, etc.)*. These tasks are called major tree headings and are the first or broadest level of detail on the Tree Diagram.

➠ Place these three to four tasks *(listed on the 3" x 5" cards or sticky notes)* immediately to the right of the statement or goal you identified in Step 1.

Note: These tasks will now become your group's focal point.

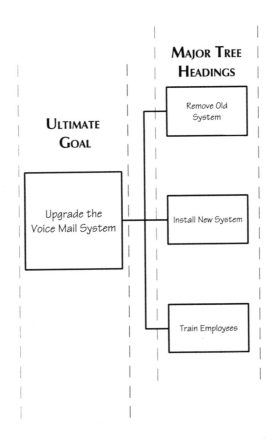

Diagram # 3 - Identify major tree headings

After the team had an opportunity to review . . .

all the brainstormed tasks, Frank asked them to pick out three or four major tasks that could be viewed as the most important elements of implementing a new voice mail system. The team was having trouble determining these tasks (*i.e., major tree headings*) until Frank described them as larger, overall steps that would include all of the smaller tasks.

After ten minutes of conversation, the group decided that the three major steps for implementing the new system were: removing the old system, installing the new system, and training employees on the new system. The team chose these three because all of the other brainstormed tasks seemed to fall under them (*see Diagram # 3*). . . .

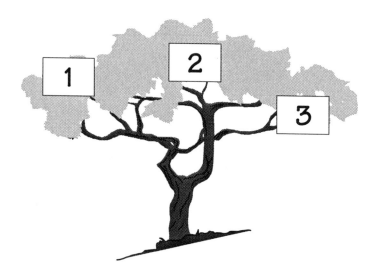

Step 4: Create The Next Level Of Detail

The major tree headings you chose in the previous step now become subgoals. All the other brainstormed tasks that fall under these tree headings should help you reach these subgoals.

Note: It may be necessary to brainstorm additional tasks at this point.

Select the tasks that must be accomplished in order to reach the subgoals, and line them up to the right of the appropriate major tree heading (*subgoal*). These tasks should be in sequential order.

Hint: Ask the question: What tasks do we need to complete to get to the major tree heading (*subgoal*)?

Continue this process until all levels of detail are arranged on the Tree Diagram (*i.e., all individual tasks are sorted and placed appropriately on the Tree Diagram*).

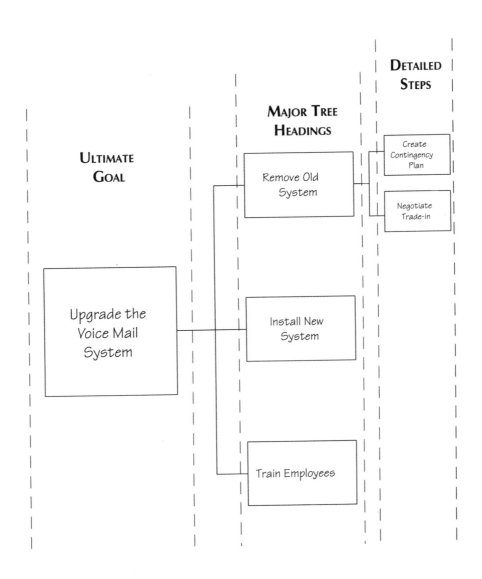

Diagram # 4 - The next level of detail

Frank asked the group . . .

to think about the three major tree headings and consider what tasks needed to be completed before the three subgoals would be reached. As the group began to sort the remaining sticky notes into the three categories, tasks that had been missed were written down. Some of the tasks that fell under removing the old system included: notifying all users two to three weeks in advance, creating a contingency plan for any downtime, negotiating a trade-in for the old system, etc.

Frank reiterated the question, *"What tasks do we need to accomplish to reach the major tree headings?"* This helped the group focus on sequencing and identifying specific tasks. As Penny began rearranging the tasks, she made sure that the Tree Diagram was built with the broadest level of detail on the left side, while the specific tasks that would lead to completing the broad level (*i.e., the first things to be done*) appeared on the right side of the diagram (*see Diagram # 4*). . . .

Step 5: Review The Tree Diagram

Check for any gaps in logic, or things that just don't make sense, on your Tree Diagram. Do this by reviewing each *"branch."* Start at the far right of the diagram, since these are the tasks that need to be completed first.

Hint: To check the sequence of tasks, ask the question: *"If we complete this task, will it lead us to the next task on the Tree Diagram?"*

➠ Additional activities, above and beyond checking for gaps in logic, can be accomplished in this step. For example, you could review the Tree Diagram with other groups or departments to get different viewpoints.

➠ Revise the Tree Diagram if your review necessitates changes.

➠ Make any necessary action assignments (*e.g., communicate responsibilities, clarify responsibilities, etc.*).

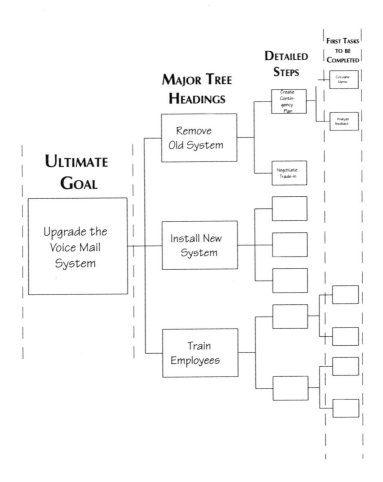

Diagram # 5 - Getting down to specifics

After the team arranged all of the sticky notes . . .

sequentially on the flip chart, it was time to review the diagram and check for gaps in logic. The team members reviewed each individual task on the Tree Diagram, always keeping in mind the question: *"If we complete this task, will it lead us to the next one on the Tree Diagram?"* During this process, the team added another level of tasks to break the steps down into more specific and detailed subtasks *(see Diagram # 5)*. After this review was completed, Frank suggested that other voice mail users be invited to the next meeting to review and check for gaps in the diagram. . . .

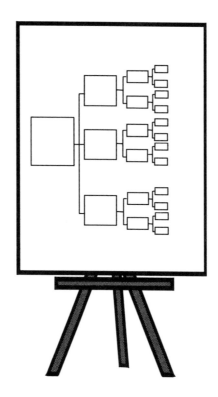

Decide On Next Steps

Once your Tree Diagram has been reviewed by team members, different departments, customers, and suppliers, additional steps need to be determined.

Possible next steps include:

➠ Assigning responsibility to carry out tasks

➠ Setting deadlines

➠ Deciding on measurements to determine the effectiveness of the corrective action

Based on the input from the other voice mail users . . .

that attended the second meeting, several changes and additions were made to the original Tree Diagram. Frank asked for volunteers to carry out some of the specific first tasks that needed to be tackled, and he set up a subteam to create an overall implementation time line. With those assignments made, the team agreed they now had a good *"road map"* to begin their implementation process.

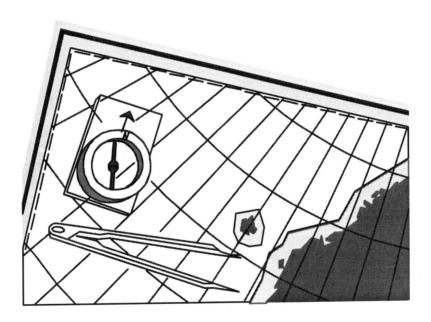

In summary, use the Tree Diagram when:

☑ You and your team need to create an implementation plan for a complex project. Note that the Tree Diagram can be time consuming and tedious, and may not be necessary for relatively simple projects.

☑ The potential negative outcomes from missing a step are large (*i.e., legal, safety-related steps or not meeting customer requirements*).

☑ Your team has stalled at the implementation step and is confused about what to do next. The Tree Diagram provides a step-by-step process for creating an implementation plan.

☑ Your team is losing its focus. The Tree Diagram focuses your team on one main goal.

☑ There is a question about the sequence of tasks that need to be completed. Creating the Tree Diagram forces a team to think about and agree on the sequence of tasks for a project.

☑ Your team wants to check the logic of an implementation plan. A completed Tree Diagram will show potential gaps in a plan.

CHAPTER TWO WORKSHEET:
TREE DIAGRAM—IDEAS FOR USE

1. List your specific opportunities to use Tree Diagrams in your organization.

2. How many levels of detailed steps are appropriate in these situations?

3. How would you use a Tree Diagram to communicate to others in your organization your plans?

PARETO CHART

The Pareto Chart is a special type of bar graph you can use as an interpretation tool in:

☞ **Determining the relative frequency or importance of different problems or causes**

☞ **Focusing on vital issues by ranking them in terms of significance**

Note: Before you can construct a Pareto Chart, you need to know how to use Check Sheets *(since the data you collect with the Check Sheet will be used to construct the Pareto Chart; see Continuous Improvement Tools Volume 1)* and other basic data-gathering tools.

Creating a Pareto Chart consists of five major steps:

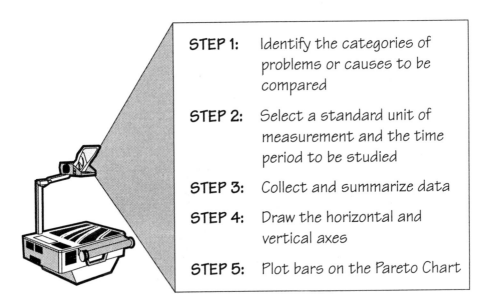

STEP 1: Identify the categories of problems or causes to be compared

STEP 2: Select a standard unit of measurement and the time period to be studied

STEP 3: Collect and summarize data

STEP 4: Draw the horizontal and vertical axes

STEP 5: Plot bars on the Pareto Chart

The example that follows shows how the Pareto Chart is used to help distinguish opinion from fact.

> ## *Yvonne, Correspondence Center Supervisor, . . .*
> had been hearing from the center's internal customers about frequent typos and misspellings in documents created by the Center, and she wanted the *"problems"* corrected. Yvonne and Tony, an Administrative Assistant, decided that a Pareto Chart would help them pinpoint the specific problems and their cause(s). . . .

Step 1: Identify The Categories Of Problems Or Causes To Be Compared

Begin by organizing the problems or causes into a handful of categories. Narrow down a long list to a manageable number of eight categories or less.

For example, if you are measuring reasons why you were late to work over a period of time, possible categories could consist of: too busy, traffic, oversleeping, arguing with your spouse or children, etc.

Note: This information can be obtained from brainstorming, a Cause and Effect Diagram, Check Sheets, existing reports, data, etc.

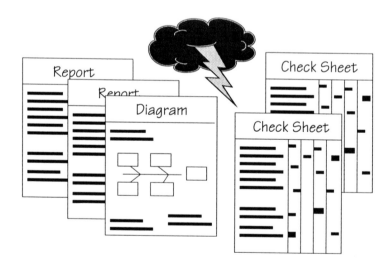

> ## *Yvonne called together a small group of people . . .*
> who had been on the receiving end of some of the Center's errors. She asked them to brainstorm a list of errors they had noticed in the last few months.

Yvonne then asked the group to identify five error categories. The categories chosen were: punctuation errors, keystroke errors, spelling errors, late deliveries, and wrong page numbering. . . .

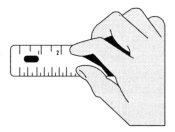

Step 2: Select A Standard Unit Of Measurement And The Time Period To Be Studied

The measurement you select will depend on the type of situation you are working with. It could be a measure of how often something occurs (*such as defects, errors, overflows, cost overruns, etc.*), how often reasons are cited in surveys as the cause of a certain problem, or a specific measurement of volume or size.

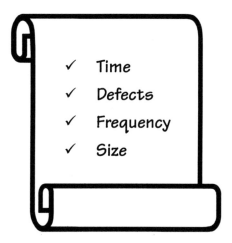

✓   Time

✓   Defects

✓   Frequency

✓   Size

Note: When selecting a sample time period, allow a long enough span to gather the required data. For example, if you were measuring reasons why people get to work late, you would not use data gathered from just one day of the week. On Monday, traffic might be heavier than Tuesday or Wednesday. By spanning a week or more, any special cases, such as Monday morning traffic, will balance out against the other reasons why people are late to work.

Yvonne gave Tony the go-ahead . . .

to collect data and build the Pareto Chart. Tony had been in a training session the month before and learned that measuring the right variable on the chart gave him valid insight. He began tracking all errors in a 30-day span—a long enough time period to get a clear picture of what was going on. Tony realized the customers were not reporting all of the errors to the Center. He personally contacted each customer requesting they report all errors. Tony even mailed each customer special cards to record this information. When he explained to them that the information gathered would reduce errors, they were only too happy to help! . . .

Date:_____

Error: _____

_____

Error: _____

_____

Step 3: Collect And Summarize Data

Begin by creating a three-column table, for which the headings should be *"error category," "frequency,"* and *"percent of total."* The items in the *"error category"* column should include the different types of errors *(or causes of errors)* that occur. This information can be taken directly from your Check Sheets.

Under the *"frequency"* column, write in the totals for each of the categories.

Now divide each number in the *"frequency"* column by the total number of measurements. This will give you the percentage of the total. For example, if the frequency for a given category is 30, and the total measurements add up to 80, the percentage *(30/80)* equals 37.5%. Write your calculated percentage under the heading entitled *"percent of total"* for each category.

ERROR CATEGORY	FREQUENCY	PERCENT OF TOTAL
Punctuation	20	44%
Keystroke	12	27%
Spelling	7	16%
Late	5	11%
Page #'s	1	2%
TOTAL	45	100%

Diagram # 6 - Create a data table

Tony started by creating a table . . .

for the data he had collected during the past month *(see Diagram # 6)*. He listed the various errors made under the category column. Tony then recorded the frequency of each error in the second column *(this information was obtained directly from the Check Sheets)*. Finally, he calculated the percentage of total errors for each of the categories and recorded those in the appropriate spaces. Tony was now ready to draw his Pareto Chart. . . .

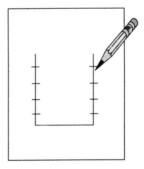

Step 4: Draw The Horizontal And Vertical Axes

Begin by drawing the horizontal axis. Draw a line from left to right on a piece of paper. Make the line long enough so all the categories can be written under it. Write the categories in descending order with the most frequently occurring category on the far left *(or beginning of the horizontal line)*. Label the axis. The label should tell the readers what they are looking at *(e.g., causes for being late to work, types of customer complaints, etc.)*.

Next draw a vertical line up from the far left point of the horizontal axis. This line will indicate the frequency for each of the categories. Scale it so the value at the top of the axis is slightly higher than the highest frequency number. Label this axis also. Again, the label should tell the readers what they are looking at (*i.e., frequency of occurrence*).

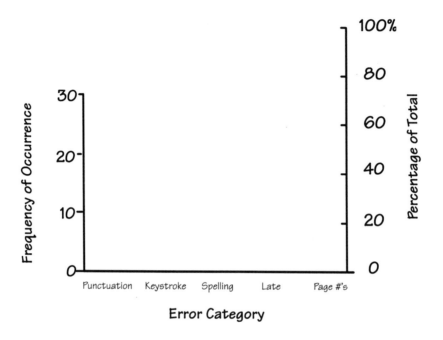

Diagram # 7 - Organize the Pareto Chart

Draw another vertical axis, this time from the far right side of the horizontal axis. This line will represent the percentage scale and should be scaled so that the point for the number of occurrences on the left matches with the corresponding percentage on the right.

Tony drew the horizontal and vertical axes . . .

He labeled the horizontal axis *"Error Category,"* and the vertical axes *"Frequency of Occurrence"* and *"Percentage of Total."* Since punctuation errors occurred most frequently, Tony made *"punctuation"* the first category on the far left. He wrote in *"keystroke"* as the next category on the axis and so on (*see Diagram # 7*) . . . .

Step 5: Plot Bars On The Pareto Chart

The final step is to plot the data by drawing a series of bars in decreasing height from left to right, using the frequency scale on the left vertical axis.

Note: Categories with very few items can be combined into an *"Other"* or *"Miscellaneous"* category, which is placed on the extreme right of the last bar.

To plot the cumulative percentage line, place a dot above each bar at a height corresponding to the scale on the right vertical axis. Starting with the first column on the left, draw a line to connect these dots from left to right, ending with the 100% point at the top of the right vertical axis.

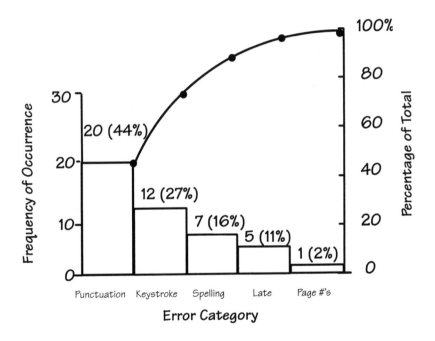

Diagram # 8 - Plot the data

While Tony plotted the chart, . . .

the biggest issues became clear. Two sources, punctuation and wrong key-strokes, together accounted for 71% of the problem. Tony and Yvonne de-cided to create a game plan before presenting the chart to the rest of the Correspondence Center *(see Diagram # 8)*. . . .

Follow-up: Decide On The Next Steps

You now have an easy-to-read and understand chart that should
help you decide what to tackle first. While working on your problems (*e.g., customer complaints, etc.*), however, continue to investigate. For example, just because a certain problem occurs most often
doesn't necessarily mean it demands your greatest attention. Also
consider the following:

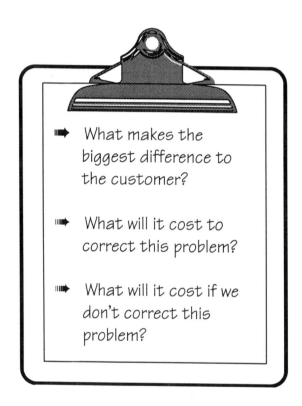

> ➡ What makes the
>   biggest difference to
>   the customer?
>
> ➡ What will it cost to
>   correct this problem?
>
> ➡ What will it cost if we
>   don't correct this
>   problem?

Investigating all the angles will help you decide which problem
should be worked on first.

Remember, while your data will lead you in a certain direction, the
customer should have the final say on what should be corrected
first. Continue to collect and plot data to verify your original
findings, and also to evaluate any changes (*improvements*) you
make.

Priorities per Pareto Chart	Priorities per Customer
1. Punctuation (44%)	1. Late deliveries
2. Keystroke (27%)	
3. Spelling (16%)	
4. Late deliveries (11%)	
5. Wrong page #'s (2%)	

Having completed his Pareto Chart, . . .

Tony reviewed the data with Yvonne and agreed to share it with a cross section of the Correspondence Center's internal customers. This meeting provided new insight. The number one complaint for several of the Center's key customers was material not being completed on time. This error did not happen often, but when it did, customers experienced severe problems *(e.g., missed deadlines, rescheduled meetings, additional work hours, etc.)*.

Tony discovered firsthand that although the data highlighted one finding *(i.e., punctuation errors are the biggest problem)*, the customers' perspective was completely different *(i.e., "get the material to us on time")*. Based on this information, Tony, Yvonne, and a cross section of the Correspondence Center's workers and customers, created an improvement team to focus on eliminating work being delivered late from the Correspondence Center.

SUMMARY

In summary, use the Pareto Chart when:

☑ You or your team need to select a problem or process to improve (*i.e., which problem occurs most often. Remember, the most frequent problem isn't necessarily the problem that should be worked on*).

☑ You or your team need to evaluate improvement efforts that you have already made (*to show if things are improving or not*).

☑ You or your team want to identify the distribution of the cause(s) of a problem (*i.e., prioritizing the causes from most to least significant*).

CHAPTER THREE WORKSHEET: PARETO CHART—IDEAS FOR USE

1. What specific opportunities do you have in your organization to use Pareto Charts?

_____

_____

2. What needs to be measured to gather the necessary data?

_____

_____

3. How might Pareto Charts help make decisions and communicate to others the specific situations you identified above?

Situation: _____

Making Decisions   Communicating to Others

• _____   • _____

• _____   • _____

Situation: _____

Making Decisions   Communicating to Others

• _____   • _____

• _____   • _____

SEQUENCE FLOW CHART

The Sequence Flow Chart is a planning and analysis tool used to:

   ↪ **Analyze the flow of work in your processes**

   ↪ **Produce a visual *"picture"* of a process, making it easy for people to understand, discuss, and communicate**

   ↪ **Identify opportunities for improvement in your processes**

The next chapter covers the Process Flow Chart, which is used to focus on a specific task or process. The Sequence Flow Chart is useful when analyzing a process involving several individuals or more than one department. It allows for identification of various *"customers"* and *"suppliers"* and shows how and when they interact with each other in the process being analyzed.

Completing a Sequence Flow Chart requires eight steps:

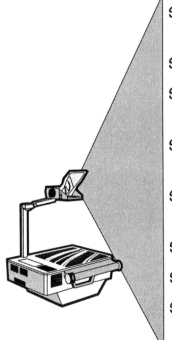

STEP 1: Prepare for the Sequence Flow Chart session

STEP 2: Identify process tasks

STEP 3: Identify people involved with the process

STEP 4: Determine customers and suppliers for each task

STEP 5: Determine "time-per-task" and "elapsed time"

STEP 6: Identify feedback loops

STEP 7: Analyze the process

STEP 8: Wrap up the Sequence Flow Chart session

The following example reveals how one team used the Sequence Flow Chart to successfully define and analyze a major process.

Larry, an Accounts Payable Analyst, . . .

needed to come up with an idea fast. His annual review was approaching and one of the review requirements stipulated he was to improve at least one process. *"This is all I need,"* Larry grumbled. *"Everyone is breathing down my neck for expense reimbursements, and now I have to do one of these improvement projects. I just don't have time."*

Larry's supervisor, Val, suggested he coordinate a team to try to improve the expense report and reimbursement process. Larry thought, *"Why not? At least I know the process, and people do complain about how long it takes. Maybe I can streamline it and get people off my back . . . ."*

Step 1: Prepare For The Sequence Flow Chart Session

Prior to beginning your Sequence Flow Chart session:

Create the Sequence Flow Chart worksheet. This worksheet is an instrument the team will use to record many different items: process tasks, people or departments involved in completing the process tasks, time-per-task, elapsed time, and any improvement opportunities identified during the session *(see Diagram # 9)*.

SEQUENCE FLOW CHART WORKSHEET

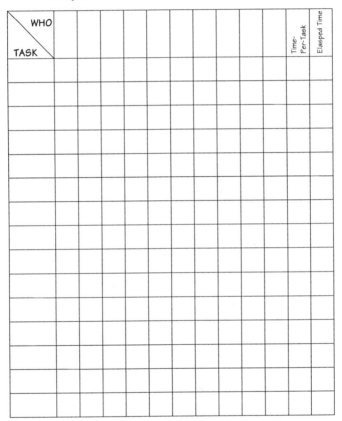

Diagram # 9 - Create the Sequence Flow Chart worksheet

Ask team members to list all tasks in the process as prework for the session. This assignment will prepare the members for the work at hand.

Provide a time limit for the session. Generally, the first session should last 50-60 minutes. Creating the Sequence Flow Chart will likely require more than one session.

Identify a Recorder for the session *(this person should have some knowledge of the Sequence Flow Chart process).*

Larry called together three other analysts . . .

and two of the biggest users of the expense reimbursement process *(i.e., the department's internal customers)* for a one-hour meeting to kick off the Sequence Flow Chart process. The company had recently gone through process-improvement training, and everyone was relatively familiar with how to create a Sequence Flow Chart. . . .

Step 2: Identify Process Tasks

The goal of this step is to list all process tasks in order *(hence the name—Sequence Flow Chart).* If your team members come prepared *(see Step # 1),* this step is much easier and less time-consuming.

Before you begin listing the tasks, it is crucial to identify process boundaries. Process boundaries act as guides in determining when a process starts and when it stops. The process starts when you *(your team, your work group, etc.)* receive an input *(an input can be an order form, a subassembly, a document of any kind, etc.).* It ends when you hand the item to the next process *(or the end user).* Boundaries need to be identified so you can focus your activity on a specific, clearly defined process.

As tasks are identified by the group, the Recorder should write them on the Sequence Flow Chart worksheet. This form is more than likely on an overhead transparency or a flip chart.

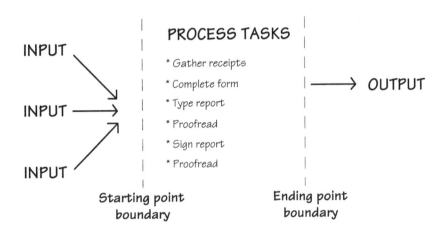

Note: It is helpful to leave a blank line in between the process tasks in case tasks are missed.

When describing tasks, write them in a verb-noun combination *(e.g., deliver material, review accuracy, complete form, solder connection).* This helps describe the exact activity that takes place during a specific task.

Write out process tasks as they actually occur as opposed to how they should occur. Real improvements can only be made with a true understanding of process, so accuracy is critical.

SEQUENCE FLOW CHART WORKSHEET

WHO / TASK													Time-Per-Task	Elapsed Time
Gather Receipts														
Complete Form														
Type Report														
Proofread														
Sign Report														
Proofread														
Request Approval														
Approve/ Reject														
Forward to Coordinator														
Proofread														
Forward to Accounting														
Reconcile Amounts														

Diagram # 10 - Identify process tasks

Larry volunteered to record . . .

the process tasks on the Sequence Flow Chart worksheet. He provided an overhead transparency of the form so the group could see the tasks as he wrote them. The group was familiar with the expense report process so prework was not necessary. The group members decided to set the beginning boundary of the process at the point of filling out the expense report form. That way they could get an idea of what happens every step of the way. Larry began by writing the first step of the process: *"gather receipts."* After some discussion about what really happened next, the group began to list the remaining tasks *(see Diagram # 10)*. . . .

Step 3: Identify People Involved With The Process

Along the top of the Sequence Flow Chart form, list the various individuals, departments, work teams, or suppliers that have ownership or are customers of the listed tasks. These individuals or groups can be referred to as *"players"* in the process.

Larry

Task 2

The group had identified 12 major tasks . . .

necessary to complete an expense report. The Sequence Flow Chart reflected how things really happened. The group realized that no specific procedure existed; therefore many versions of the process were possible. Larry then asked for the individuals, departments, work teams, suppliers, and customers who carry out the identified tasks. *"Players"* included secretaries, supervisors, the travel department, and accounts payable. All were listed across the top of the form *(see Diagram # 11). . . .*

SEQUENCE FLOW CHART WORKSHEET

WHO TASK	Employee		Secretary		Supervisor		Travel Coordinator		Accounting		Time-Per-Task	Elapsed Time
Gather Receipts												
Complete Form												
Type Report												
Proofread												
Sign Report												
Proofread												
Request Approval												
Approve/ Reject												
Forward to Coordinator												
Proofread												
Forward to Accounting												
Reconcile Amounts												

Diagram # 11 - Who's involved in the process

Step 4: Determine Customers And Suppliers For Each Task

You need to identify the customers and suppliers for each task in the process. Code each of the tasks with the appropriate symbol *(either customer, supplier, shared responsibility, or may or may not be involved—see Diagram # 12)* for the individual, department, or work teams listed at the top of the Sequence Flow Chart worksheet.

Diagram # 12 - Sequence Flow Chart Symbols

After identifying the key "players," . . .

Larry and his group coded each *"player"* as a supplier or customer, having shared responsibility, or possible involvement or not, depending on the circumstances. Larry noted it was important for each task to have only one primary supplier and to clarify who owned the step *(see Diagram # 13)*. Sixty minutes had passed, and the group had a good start on their Sequence Flow Chart. The next steps would involve determining time-per-task and elapsed time as well as identifying any feedback loops. Larry asked the two group members who were expense report users to identify time-per-task and the elapsed time prior to the team's next get-together, while he and his coworkers agreed to rethink the process and look for redundancies. . . .

SEQUENCE FLOW CHART WORKSHEET

WHO \ TASK	Employee		Secretary		Supervisor		Travel Coordinator		Accounting		Time-Per-Task	Elapsed Time
Gather Receipts	●											
Complete Form	●		✗									
Type Report			●									
Proofread	✗		●									
Sign Report	●											
Proofread	●											
Request Approval	●				✗							
Approve/Reject	✗				●							
Forward to Coordinator	●						✗					
Proofread							●					
Forward to Accounting							●		✗			
Reconcile Amounts	✗								●			

Diagram # 13 - Customers and suppliers for each step

Step 5: Determine *"time-per-task"* and *"elapsed time"*

Each task in the process should take a certain amount of time to complete. You need to determine this *"time-per-task"* and record it in the appropriate box on the right side of the Sequence Flow Chart worksheet. By identifying the time-per-task, you can determine how long a particular series of tasks should ideally take.

Note: This is a measure of how long a process would take if no slack or down-time exists.

A series of tasks in a process takes a specified amount of time to complete. This cumulative time is termed *"elapsed time."* The elapsed time is the length of time it actually takes to complete the tasks in the process from beginning to end. Elapsed time is determined to get an indication of where slack, downtime, or bottlenecks exist in the process.

SEQUENCE FLOW CHART WORKSHEET

TASK / WHO	Employee	Secretary	Supervisor	Travel Coordinator	Accounting	Time-Per-Task	Elapsed Time
Gather Receipts	●					30	
Complete Form	●	✗				30	1 Day
Type Report		●				30	
Proofread	✗	●				10	3 Days
Sign Report	●					10	
Proofread	●					10	
Request Approval	●		✗			10	7 Days
Approve/ Reject	✗		●			10	10 Days
Forward to Coordinator	●			✗		10	11 Days
Proofread				●		10	
Forward to Accounting				●	✗	10	12 Days
Reconcile Amounts	✗				●	90	20 Days
TOTAL						4.3 Hrs.	20 Days

Diagram # 14 - Total "time-per-task" and "elapsed time"

At the beginning of the next meeting, . . .

Larry reviewed the Sequence Flow Chart and asked for the time-per-task and elapsed time information. Donna and Richard, who had compiled the information, were shocked at the difference between the actual time-per-task and the cumulative time the process actually took, or elapsed time. The group decided there was a significant opportunity for cycle-time reduction; they only had to determine where they could make the reductions (*see Diagram #14*). . . .

Step 6: Identify Feedback Loops

You can use feedback loops to identify areas in a process where redundancies or repetitive tasks take place. Feedback loops are placed on your Sequence Flow Chart at the point where process tasks have to be redone. Identify the feedback loop by drawing a dashed line on the Sequence Flow Chart connecting the task begining the loop with the first task needing to be redone.

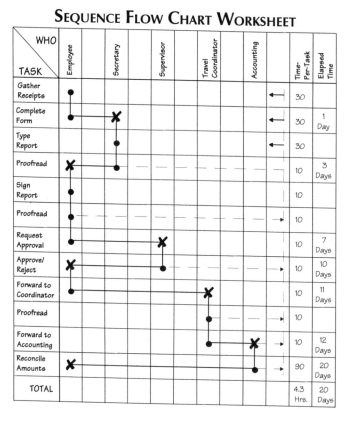

SEQUENCE FLOW CHART WORKSHEET

WHO / TASK	Employee	Secretary	Supervisor	Travel Coordinator	Accounting		Time-Per-Task	Elapsed Time
Gather Receipts	●					←	30	
Complete Form	●	X				←	30	1 Day
Type Report		●				←	30	
Proofread	X	●					10	3 Days
Sign Report	●						10	
Proofread	●					→	10	
Request Approval	●		X				10	7 Days
Approve/ Reject	X		●			→	10	10 Days
Forward to Coordinator	●			X			10	11 Days
Proofread				●		→	10	
Forward to Accounting				●	X	→	10	12 Days
Reconcile Amounts	X				●	→	90	20 Days
TOTAL							4.3 Hrs.	20 Days

Diagram # 15 - Sequence Flow Chart with feedback loops

The group members . . .

added feedback loops to identify several areas in the process where redundancies existed. These areas turned out to be ideal measurement opportunities. Eliminating or reducing them would help lower cycle time, which, in turn, would save money and reduce employee complaints about the process taking too long (*see Diagram # 15*).

Step 7: Analyze The Process

Including time-per-task, elapsed time, and feedback loops on your Sequence Flow Chart will allow you a greater opportunity to analyze your process. Looking at the differences between time-per-task and elapsed *(or cumulative)* time will help you see where *"hold-ups"* in the process may exist *(see Diagram # 15)*. Once you've identified the *"holdups,"* your goal is to discover why they happen *(use the Cause and Effect Diagram, Force Field Analysis, Brainstorming, or the Affinity Diagram to help with this process)*.

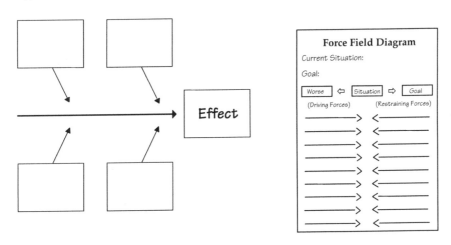

And after you've discovered the true causes, you're ready to analyze the process. The analysis should reveal whether you can reduce the elapsed time by making process improvements. Your goal, of course, is to reduce cycle time.

Feedback loops in a process *(identified by the dashed lines)* indicate repeats, or process redundancies *(see Diagram # 15)*. Whenever a feedback loop is identified *(e.g., after an inspection step, a product is rejected and requires reworking)*, it means the product *(such as a document, a subassembly, or a finished good)* has to go backwards in the process and repeat a number of process steps *(the dashed feedback loop will show how many steps must be repeated)*. For every feedback loop identified on the Sequence Flow Chart, you need to measure how often the redundancy occurs. By taking measurements, you know exactly how much work you are redoing *(and you also know where your improvements have had a positive effect!)*.

Step 8: Wrap Up the Sequence Flow Chart Session

You know it's time to end your Sequence Flow Chart session when:

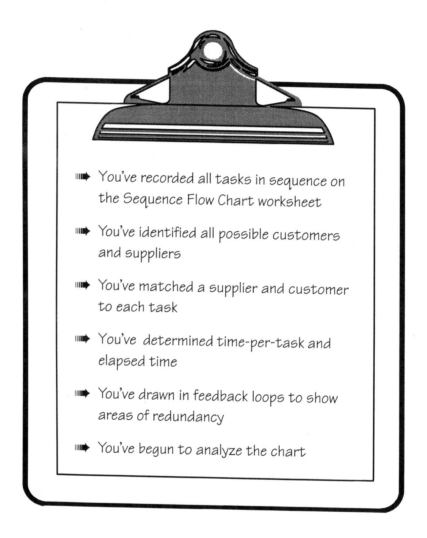

⮕ You've recorded all tasks in sequence on the Sequence Flow Chart worksheet

⮕ You've identified all possible customers and suppliers

⮕ You've matched a supplier and customer to each task

⮕ You've determined time-per-task and elapsed time

⮕ You've drawn in feedback loops to show areas of redundancy

⮕ You've begun to analyze the chart

Follow-up: Decide On Next Steps

You now have a chart showing exactly what happens in a work process. If you included everyone involved in or affected by the process when you developed the chart, you probably have a consensus that the Sequence Flow Chart is accurate. The next steps should build on the momentum you've created.

These steps might include:

➠ Getting further input from others, if necessary

➠ Eliminating certain steps in the process

➠ Identifying which redundancies can be eliminated and how

➠ Setting specific targets for reducing the gap between total task time (sum of the times-per-task) and elapsed time

➠ Setting target dates for achieving these lower gaps

With the Sequence Flow Chart completed, . . .

Larry and his group felt they could make real improvements in cycle time and in employee *(internal customer)* satisfaction. Several steps in the process could be eliminated or changed. Larry's supervisor empowered the group to make changes, so they decided to test potential improvements *(e.g., eliminating the typing and the first proofreading step of the expense report process)* in one department. Larry felt confident he had not only met the requirement for his review, but had also made his job easier.

In summary, use the Sequence Flow Chart when:

☑ You are working with a service-related process. The Sequence Flow Chart may be more appropriate when processes are cross-functional and involve more individuals.

☑ You and your team need to define the steps in a process. One of the first things to do when analyzing a process is to list the steps.

☑ You are trying to determine areas for improvement in a process. The Sequence Flow Chart will help you or your team identify process redo's and opportunities for cycle-time reduction.

☑ You are trying to create a new process. Once completed, the Sequence Flow Chart can become a work-process outline.

☑ You are standardizing an existing process. Different people may have different ideas about what happens in a process, the Sequence Flow Chart can help to standardize their different ideas or different methods into a simple process.

CHAPTER FOUR WORKSHEET:
SEQUENCE FLOW CHARTS—IDEAS FOR USE

1. What specific opportunities do you have in your organization to use Sequence Flow Charts?

_____

_____

_____

2. What would the goals or outcomes of these situations be?

☐ To tie together steps that cross departmental lines:

☐ To define a process:

☐ To identify improvement opportunities:

☐ To create a new process

☐ To standardize a process

3. For which existing processes are you the internal customer?

_____

_____

_____

_____

PROCESS FLOW CHART

The Process Flow Chart is a planning and analysis tool used to:

- ☞ **Define and analyze manufacturing, assembly, or service processes**

- ☞ **Build a step-by-step picture of the process for analysis, discussion, or communication purposes**

- ☞ **Define, standardize, or find areas for improvement in a process**

The Process Flow Chart focuses on a specific function or activity. Unlike the Sequence Flow Chart, it does not allow for identification of various customers and suppliers, but it is a more visual representation of a process.

Note: You may prefer the Sequence Flow Chart *(see Chapter Four)* when you need to define administrative processes because these processes often involve more individuals and will typically cross more functional lines than manufacturing processes.

Completing a Process Flow Chart consists of four major steps:

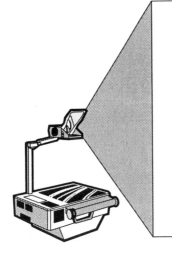

> **STEP 1:** Prepare for the Process Flow Chart session
>
> **STEP 2:** Identify major process tasks
>
> **STEP 3:** Draw the Process Flow Chart
>
> **STEP 4:** Analyze the Process Flow Chart

The example that follows shows how one team used the Process Flow Chart to successfully define and analyze a major process.

Having just completed . . .

a Process Flow Charting class the week before, Robert, a supervisor in manu-facturing, was anxious to try his new-found knowledge on a real *"live"* process. The company he worked for, Home Runners, Inc., wanted to define and evaluate their major work processes. Robert and his team *(Jane, Susan, Alfonso, and Kenny)* had been charged with defining the baseball-bat-making process for the company. And they were ready to start the first inning. . . .

Step 1: Prepare For The Process Flow Chart Session

Prior to beginning your Process Flow Chart session:

➠ Create the Process Flow Chart symbol sheet. Your Process Flow Chart symbol sheet should show all of the flow chart symbols with corresponding explanations *(see Diagram # 16)*.

➠ Provide a time limit for the session. Creating the Process Flow Chart will likely take more than one session. Generally, the first session should last 50-60 minutes.

➠ Identify a Recorder for the session. The job of the Recorder is to draw the draft flow chart as the team identifies the steps and the appropriate symbols. The person you choose should have some knowledge of Process Flow Charts.

Note: You may want to use sticky notes to help create the visual Process Flow Chart since changes may need to be made as you build it.

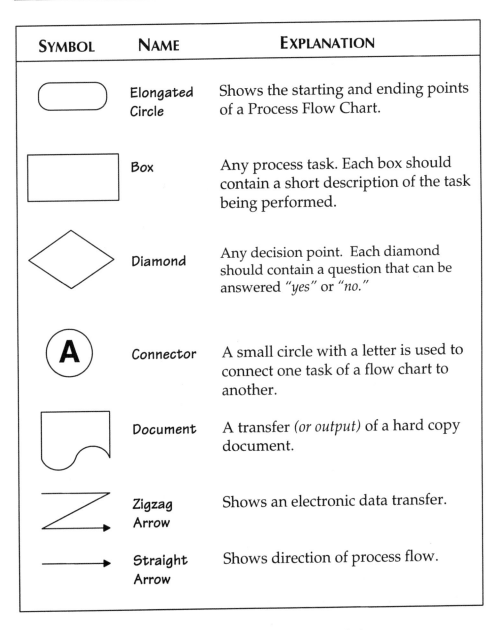

SYMBOL	NAME	EXPLANATION
	Elongated Circle	Shows the starting and ending points of a Process Flow Chart.
	Box	Any process task. Each box should contain a short description of the task being performed.
	Diamond	Any decision point. Each diamond should contain a question that can be answered *"yes"* or *"no."*
A	Connector	A small circle with a letter is used to connect one task of a flow chart to another.
	Document	A transfer *(or output)* of a hard copy document.
	Zigzag Arrow	Shows an electronic data transfer.
	Straight Arrow	Shows direction of process flow.

Diagram # 16 - Flow chart symbols

Susan, a manufacturing engineer, . . .

volunteered to be the Recorder. Robert posted the symbols they would use during the session *(see Diagram # 16)*. Susan set the expectations for the meeting by saying, *"In the next 60 minutes, let's identify the major tasks in the manufacturing process. . . . "*

Step 2: Identify Major Process Tasks

Begin your Process Flow Chart session by identifying the first major task in the process you've chosen to analyze (*this sets the boundary for the process*). After this first task has been identified, ask questions to stimulate thought and expedite the completion of the Process Flow Chart.

Suggested questions include:

⟹ What really happens next in the process?

⟹ Does a decision need to be made before the next task?

⟹ What approvals are required before moving on to the next task?

Robert said the group needed to answer...

a few questions to make sure they came up with a true picture of the process. They needed to focus on what really happened in the process, instead of what was supposed to happen, what decisions and approvals were needed, and whether anything was missing. Alfonso started by saying, "*Well, the first step is clamping the block to cut it down to size, right?*" Robert's response was, "*But don't we have to start even earlier in the process, say, at the point where we get the wood block from the storeroom?*" The group agreed, and they had their first major task. Then Kenny brought up a good point, "*How do we know it's the right size?*" Susan listed the question as a decision for the flow chart. The group continued to list decisions and process tasks (*see Diagram # 17*). . . .

Task #	Major Process Tasks	Subtasks/Decisions	Symbol
1	Receive wood block from stock	Correct size? Correct wood?	▢ ◇
2	Place into production queue		▢
3	Set up lathe for cutting	Machine ready?	▢ ◇
4	Apply holding clamps	Clamps tight?	▢ ◇
5	Get tool and cut wood block	Right cutting tool? Proper machine speed?	▢ ◇
6	Cut according to spec sheet	Wood break?	▢ ◇
7	Compare bat to spec sheet	Correct specs?	▢ ◇
8	Sign-off work order		▱
9	Forward to Finishing Dept.		▢

Diagram # 17 - List process tasks and decisions

Step 3: Draw The Process Flow Chart

Using the symbols identified in Step 1, draw the process tasks on flip chart paper or an overhead transparency. Every process will have a start and an end *(shown by an elongated circle)*. In addition, all processes will have tasks *(shown by a box)*, and most will have decision points *(shown by a diamond)*. Decision points are yes or no questions that steer the process one way or another. Tasks may also be connected to other tasks using a connector *(shown as a small circle with a letter)*. Instead of drawing long lines, the connector can be used to move to another task which may be several tasks away.

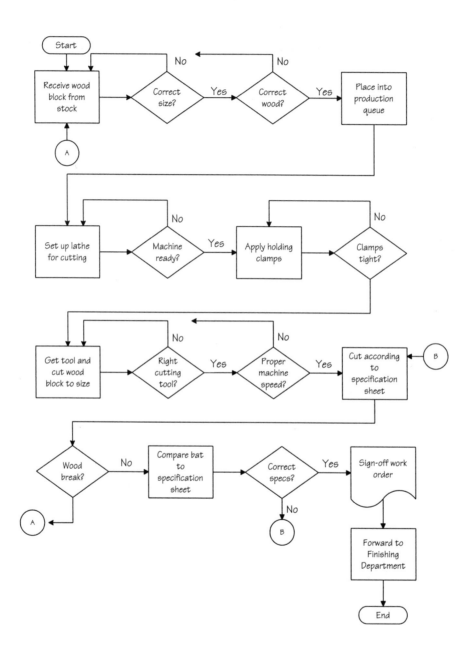

Diagram # 18 - Draw the Process Flow Chart

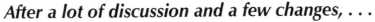
After a lot of discussion and a few changes, . . .

the group agreed to the list of tasks and were ready to draw their flow chart. Susan was elected as the resident artist and began by drawing the starting point *(identified by the elongated circle)* of their process. They agreed this was also the ending point of another flow chart—the one for storing and handling wood in the stockroom. As they were completing the flow chart, Kenny brought up a good point, *"Looking at the process this way, we can really see where all the decisions are made. For one reason or another, we're not ready to go on to the next step."* The group was getting anxious to look at ways to improve the process *(see Diagram # 18). . . .*

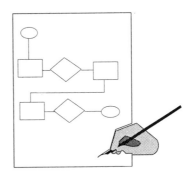

Step 4: Analyze The Process Flow Chart

The Process Flow Chart offers many opportunities for process analysis. These opportunities include analyses of:

⇒ Time-per-event *(i.e., reducing cycle time)*

⇒ Process repeats *(i.e., preventing rework)*

⇒ Duplication of effort *(i.e., identifying and eliminating duplicate tasks)*

⇒ Unnecessary tasks *(i.e., eliminating tasks that are in the process for no apparent reason)*

⇒ Value-added versus non value-added tasks

"Value-Added"

Value-added tasks are those tasks within your work process that contribute to the ability to meet and/or exceed your customers' requirements. These include activities that reduce errors, or tasks that decrease the cycle-time of a work process, such as:

Improving processes

Making "front-line" decisions

Defining measurements

Making action plans

Reviewing progress

Analyzing successes and failures

Providing feedback to suppliers

Meeting with customers

Setting goals

"Non Value-Added"

These are tasks within your work process that do not contribute to the ability to meet and/or exceed your customers' requirements. They include tasks that are unnecessary or increase the cycle time of a work process, such as:

Fixing errors but not root causes

Getting numerous approvals

Duplicating work and reports

Waiting for materials or direction

Collecting nonrelevant data

Writing reports that are not read

Going to nonproductive meetings

Reworking other people's outputs

Waiting for further instructions

Each type of analysis listed has the potential to save individuals, departments, or companies varying amounts of time *(which translates into money)* because a Process Flow Chart analysis will uncover any indication of loss or waste.

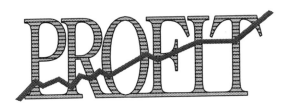

Before you make any process changes, though, you'll increase your analysis power if you first measure your current performance. This measurement will serve as a base line to determine if the changes you make to the process have a positive effect.

At the beginning of the next meeting . . .

Robert said, *"Let's look at the flow chart and see what we can learn from it."* The group spent the remaining time discussing potential process problems and areas for improvement *(e.g., unnecessary steps or process redundancies).* Kenny stated that by identifying and eliminating unnecessary steps, cycle time could be reduced and money saved *(see Diagram # 18).*

"What about this decision step where we check to see if the right cutting tool is in the lathe? Maybe we can't eliminate that step, but we should be able to make it a lot easier," began Kenny. Susan continued, *"Yes, and maybe we could get the stockroom employees to change a couple of the things they do so we wouldn't have to check the size and type of wood for every block that comes in."* The group then started to look at ways to reduce or eliminate these non value-added tasks. . . .

Follow-up: Decide On Next Steps

Analyzing the Process Flow Chart is not the end of process. To fully utilize this effective tool, you need to determine what to do with your analysis.

Additional steps can include:

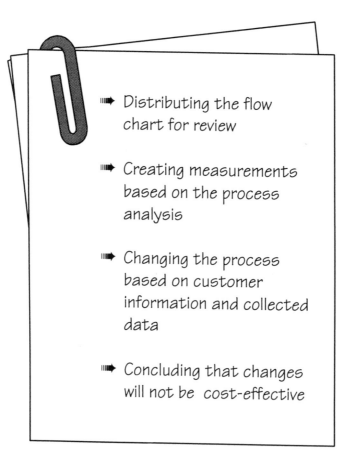

⎯⎯▸ Distributing the flow chart for review

⎯⎯▸ Creating measurements based on the process analysis

⎯⎯▸ Changing the process based on customer information and collected data

⎯⎯▸ Concluding that changes will not be cost-effective

Action Items

■ Distribute to all managers

■ Collect customer data

■ Focus on problem areas
—next meeting

After completing an initial analysis of the process, . . .

Susan volunteered to take the flip chart information and make a printout for all managers to review. Robert said, *"We should focus our next meeting around problem areas, or areas for improvement"* (e.g., *unnecessary steps, or process redundancies*). Kenny suggested the group collect customer information about internal and external customer requirements. Alfonso suggested using a survey he had created. The ideas were coming fast and furious, so Jane used the flip chart to record the *"action items."* Robert was pleased with the team's performance and was excited about the possibility of improvements. The Process Flow Chart really did make a difference.

SUMMARY

In summary, use the Process Flow Chart when:

☑ You and your team are working with a service, manufacturing, or assembly-related process. The Process Flow Chart may be more appropriate when focusing on a specific function or task, and when the identification of various customers and suppliers is not crucial.

☑ You and your team need to define the tasks in a process.

☑ You are trying to determine areas for improvement in a process. The Process Flow Chart will help you and your team identify process redundancies and other problem areas.

☑ You and your team are designing a new process. The Process Flow Chart will provide a visual representation of the process.

☑ You and your team are standardizing an existing process. The Process Flow Chart will clarify differing viewpoints concerning the activity in a process.

CHAPTER FIVE WORKSHEET:
PROCESS FLOW CHART—IDEAS FOR USE

1. What specific opportunities do you have in your organization to use Process Flow Charts?

    _____

    _____

    _____

2. Who will be involved in the Flow Chart creation process? Why?

    Situation:_____

    Who:_____

    Why:_____

    Situation:_____

    Who:_____

    Why:_____

3. What would you be analyzing in the process (*e.g., time involved, redundancies, repeats, etc.*)?

    _____

    _____

    _____

SCATTER DIAGRAM

The Scatter Diagram is a data interpretation tool used to:

⇝ **Examine how strong the relationship is between two variables** *(e.g., the relationship between advertising costs and sales, years of experience and employee performance, etc.)*

⇝ **Confirm** *"hunches"* **about a direct cause-and-effect relationship between types of variables**

⇝ **Determine the type of relationship** *(positive, negative, etc.)*

Scatter Diagrams are easy to use, and the results are easy to understand. This tool can be adapted for use in many types of situations.

The Scatter Diagram consists of four major steps:

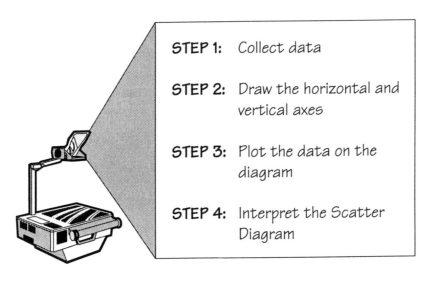

STEP 1: Collect data

STEP 2: Draw the horizontal and vertical axes

STEP 3: Plot the data on the diagram

STEP 4: Interpret the Scatter Diagram

The example that follows illustrates how the Scatter Diagram is used to interpret data.

The Training Department . . .

was beginning to feel the heat. Suzy, the Training Manager, had recently implemented a number of quality-related courses. Now she was asked to prove that they were working. Suzy called a department meeting to discuss the dilemma. Carla, a Training Specialist, thought the Scatter Diagram would be a good way to visualize the positive impact of the quality-related training. After all, their department trained people to use the Scatter Diagram. Couldn't they use it just as effectively? . . .

Step 1: Collect Data

Collect 25 to 50 *(no more than 100)* data points for each variable you are studying. Create a Summary Check Sheet showing the specific data for each variable *(i.e., the things being compared)*.

SUMMARY CHECK SHEET

Employee	Training Hours	Successful Improvements
1	0	1
2	1	1
3	10	6
4	12	8
50	2	1

Diagram # 19 - Collect data

Carla and Don volunteered to research . . .

a cross section of 50 training participants to determine how many hours of class they had attended, and how many successful process-improvement efforts they had contributed. After researching 50 participants, Carla and Don created a table containing 50 data points relating quality-training hours and successful process improvements *(see Diagram # 19)*. . . .

Step 2: Draw The Horizontal And Vertical Axes

To draw your Scatter Diagram, follow these steps:

⟶ Draw the horizontal (X), and the vertical (Y) axes.

⟶ Name the axes.

> **Note:** It is common for the *"cause"* variable *(i.e. the event that triggers or causes something else to happen)* to be on the horizontal axis and the *"effect"* variable *(i.e. what happens in response to the cause variable)* on the vertical axis *(see Diagram # 20).*

⟶ Add scales to the axes.

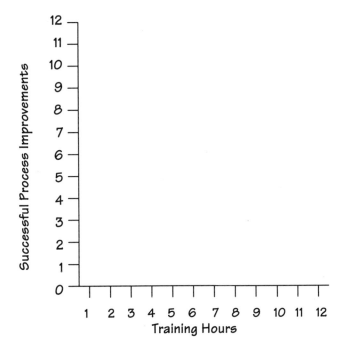

Diagram # 20 - Draw the Scatter Diagram

Don noted that the Scatter Diagram . . .

begins like any line graph. He drew the horizontal and vertical axes. After scanning the table, he observed the numbers did not go over 12, so 12 became the highest value on each axis. Don labeled the horizontal (X) axis with the cause variable—training hours, and the vertical (Y) axis with the effect variable—successful process improvements *(see Diagram # 20)*. . . .

Step 3: Plot The Data On The Diagram

For each data point, find the intersections of the variables on the Scatter Diagram and then plot each point. If you have two or more identical data points, circle the point as many times as appropriate.

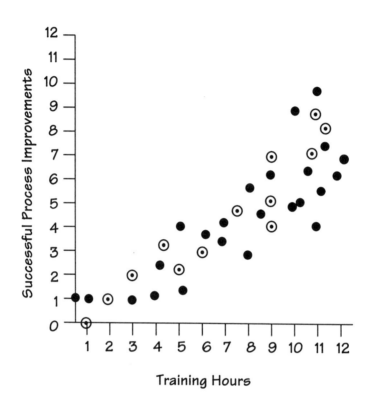

Diagram # 21 - Plot the data

Plotting the data . . .

went faster than Don thought it would. *"This is easy,"* he said to himself. *"All I have to do is find the intersection of the number of training hours and the number of successful process improvements for each participant, and then plot the point."* For repeated intersections, Don circled the point as many times as was appropriate *(see Diagram # 21). . . .*

Step 4: Interpret The Scatter Diagram

When you interpret the Scatter Diagram, it's important to remember that only *possible* causal relationships are shown, not *actual* causal relationships. More advanced statistical tests are necessary if you want to determine the exact degree of the relationship.

Don and Carla presented the Scatter Diagram . . .

at the next department meeting. Suzy was pleased that there appeared to be a clear positive causal relationship between training hours and successful process improvements *(i.e., the more training hours utilized, the higher the amount of successful process improvements)*. Having tangible data in hand, she now felt assured the new quality training was a real success. She asked Don to keep the diagram updated so they could see any changes in the effectiveness of the quality training. . . .

The following is a sample of possible data patterns, and what those patterns mean.

Positive Relationship: An increase in Y is caused by an increase in X. If we control X, we generally can control Y *(see Diagram # 21A).*

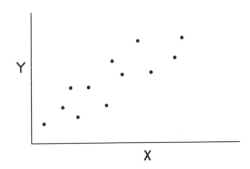

Diagram # 21A - Positive relationship

Possible Positive Relationship: An increase in X seems to increase Y, but Y has other possible causes *(see Diagram # 21B).*

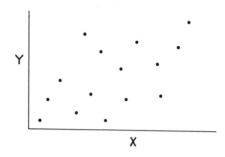

Diagram # 21B - Possible positive relationship

No Relationship: There is no visible relationship between X and Y *(see Diagram # 21C).*

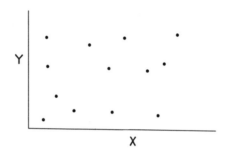

Diagram # 21C - No relationship

Possible Negative Relationship: A decrease in Y appears to be caused by an increase in X *(see Diagram # 21D).*

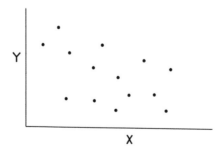

Diagram # 21D - Possible negative relationship

Negative Relationship: An increase in Y is generally caused by a decrease in X *(see Diagram # 21E)*.

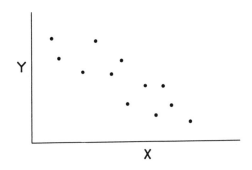

Diagram # 21E - Negative relationship

Follow-Up: Decide On The Next Steps

As with any of the improvement tools, success depends on what you do with the information you've gathered and analyzed. Some additional steps to consider after your initial interpretation of the Scatter Diagram include:

➠ Continue to collect data to verify your interpretation

➠ Make changes based on the Scatter Diagram

➠ Identify other cause variables

➠ Identify other effect variables

After the success . . .
of the first Scatter Diagram, Carla volunteered to create similar diagrams for other training programs the department offered. The rest of the department decided to try to improve the quality training further by analyzing the course evaluations and identifying areas for improvement.

In summary, use the Scatter Diagram when:

☑ You and your team want to determine the type of relationship that exists between two variables (*i.e., positive, negative, possible positive, etc.*).

☑ You and your team want to determine possible causal relationships between two variables (*e.g., the more we train our employees, the more successful process improvements we have*).

☑ You and your team want to verify and display that a relationship exists, or doesn't exist between two variables. Use the Scatter Diagram as a tracking tool to visually verify that relationships continue to exist.

Note: The statistical tests available to test the exact strength of the relationship between two variables are outside the scope of this guidebook.

CHAPTER SIX WORKSHEET:
SCATTER DIAGRAM—IDEAS FOR USE

1. What specific opportunities do you have in your organization to use Scatter Diagrams?

_____

_____

_____

2. What needs to be measured to gather the necessary data?

_____

_____

_____

3. How might the Scatter Diagram help you make decisions regarding the specific situations you identified, and then communicate them to others?

Situation:_____

Making decisions:_____

Communicating to others:_____

Situation:_____

Making decisions:_____

Communicating to others:_____

RUN CHART

The Run Chart is a type of line graph used as an analysis tool to:

- ☞ **Collect and interpret data**

- ☞ **Create a picture of what is happening in the situation you are analyzing**

- ☞ **Find patterns yielding valuable insights**

- ☞ **Compare one period of data to another, checking for changes**

The Run Chart is similar to the Scatter Diagram in that two variables are plotted against each other. However, unlike the Scatter Diagram, which is used to investigate cause and effect relationships between two variables, the Run Chart tracks changes in the variable being measured over a period of time to identify patterns.

Creating a Run Chart consists of three major steps:

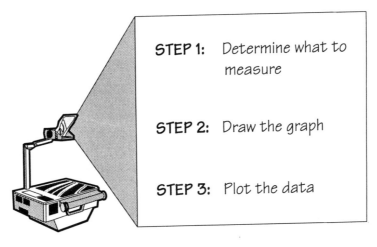

STEP 1:   Determine what to
measure

STEP 2:   Draw the graph

STEP 3:   Plot the data

The example that follows shows how one professional used the Run Chart to verify a hunch.

Danica, an Engineering Analyst, . . .

realized it was a part of life that the computer system would go down, but this was ridiculous. Twice today and four times this week it shut down, and it was only Wednesday! Danica felt a clear pattern was developing, since the *"machine"* always seemed to go down around the same time. She had used a Run Chart in the past to prove similar hunches; this seemed like the perfect opportunity to use it again. . . .

Step 1: Determine What To Measure

The first step in constructing a Run Chart is selecting one key measure to track over a period of time. This measure should be a *"quality/productivity"* (external customer or internal process) indicator providing useful information for making decisions.

Note: Measures can also be tracked against other bases, such as production batches, shifts, and so on.

Possible measures include:

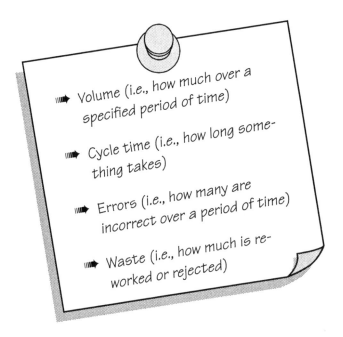

- Volume (i.e., how much over a specified period of time)

- Cycle time (i.e., how long something takes)

- Errors (i.e., how many are incorrect over a period of time)

- Waste (i.e., how much is reworked or rejected)

After you have determined what to measure, decide on the period of time during which you will collect data. Possible time intervals include: hourly, daily, weekly, monthly, quarterly, etc.

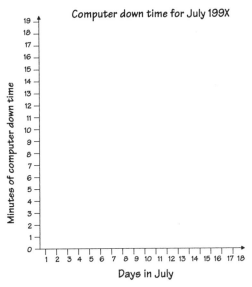

Diagram # 22 - Draw the Run Chart

Danica determined that her quality measure . . .

would be *"minutes of computer down time."* She decided to start with a daily measurement but realized the measurement may have to be changed to hourly at some point in the future. . . .

Step 2: Draw The Graph

Drawing the graph consists of three simple steps:

➥ Name the graph. The name should describe what you are measuring and the time duration you've chosen.

➥ Draw the vertical axis. The measure is always on the vertical axis, and is shown in number of occurrences or percentages.

➥ Draw the horizontal axis. The time interval or other measurement base is always shown on the horizontal axis.

With the quality measurement chosen . . .

and the time interval determined, the rest was a breeze. Danica named the graph*"Computer down time for July 199X"* and then drew the vertical and horizontal axes. She labeled the vertical axis *"Minutes of computer down time,"* and the horizontal axis *"Days in July" (see Diagram # 22). . . .*

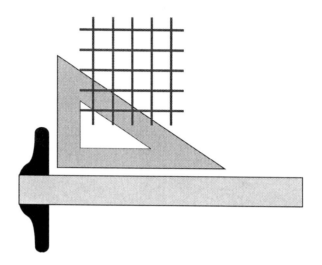

Step 3: Plot The Data

Collect data for your chosen measurement. Each data point should then be plotted on the graph in the appropriate location given its level of occurrence *(or percentage)* and time interval. If you connect the points, it will be easier to interpret the graph. Finally, calculate the average occurrence or percentage and plot that on the graph. The average line will help you to see abnormalities in the process condition *(i.e., something other than random points around the average line).*

Follow these tips for collecting and plotting data:

➠ Plot data points in the order they occur.

➠ Collect data on a regular basis *(i.e., get into a habit of collecting data at the same time and storing it in the same place).*

➠ Evaluate data on a regular basis *(i.e., post data in a place where it can be seen and reviewed by customers and suppliers).*

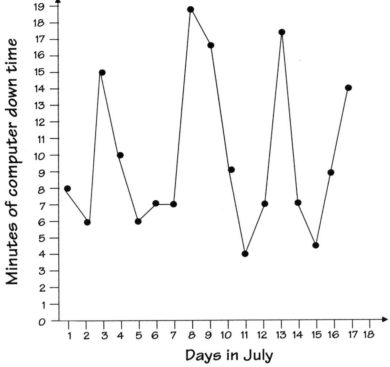

Computer down time for July 199X

Diagram # 23 - Plot the data

As the days in July went by, . . .

Danica continued to plot data on her Run Chart. The other workers in Danica's department began to take interest in the chart as the month progressed because they could finally see more down time existed than they had previously thought. Danica was careful to plot the down time as it occurred, thus ensuring the accuracy of the measurement. She also connected the data points to help her see both the trends and the extreme levels of variation in the amount of down time (*see Diagram # 23*). . . .

Follow-up: Decide On Next Steps

Once you've plotted the graph, you have the option to do one or more of the following:

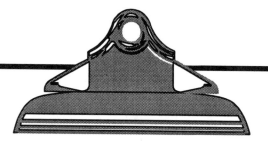

⟱ Search for patterns in the data (*e.g., errors are higher on Tuesday during the second shift*)

⟱ Determine the root cause of the error (*e.g., a new employee is working Tuesday's second shift and has not been trained yet*)

⟱ Investigate extreme highs or lows in data points (*extreme variation around the average line indicates opportunity for improvement*)

⟱ Continue measuring to track the effect of changes (*i.e., you can prove that the changes are working by tracking the data*)

⟱ Create a Control Chart to provide more information about process variation and control

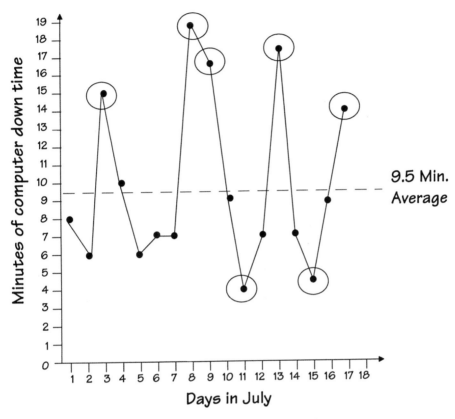

Computer down time for July 199X

Diagram # 24 - Interpret data

At the end of the month, . . .

Danica calculated the average down time and drew the line on the graph. Her original hunch seemed correct. A pattern was developing, and she decided to continue collecting data to further verify it. Also present were some extreme highs and lows in the data points on the graph (*see Diagram # 24*). This looked unusual to Danica, so she decided her next step would involve converting the Run Chart to a Control Chart. That way she could discover whether the down time was normal or whether something truly unusual was taking place.

In summary, use the Run Chart when:

☑ Trying to show trends in measurements over time or comparisons from one measurement base to another *(such as different shifts, teams, production runs, etc.)*. Since the Run Chart is always based on some comparable measurement, such as time, comparison of data is quick and easy.

☑ You need to check for long-term changes. Often data changes slowly over time. The Run Chart, if regularly updated, will show overall changes in the process average which may indicate underlying instability in process.

☑ You want to show process variations. The Run Chart will help you spot extremes in process variation.

☑ You want to evaluate changes made to the process. After improvements have been made to the process, continue to collect data using the Run Chart to verify the effectiveness of the change.

CHAPTER SEVEN WORKSHEET: RUN CHART—IDEAS FOR USE

1. What specific opportunities do you have in your organization to use Run Charts?

_____

_____

_____

_____

2. Would these situations involve tracking certain measures across time or some other base?

Yes　No

☐　☐　Time (_____daily, _____weekly,_____ monthly)

☐　☐　Batches or runs

☐　☐　Work teams (such as shifts, geographical units, etc.)

☐　☐　Other bases (specify):_____

3. Which measures would be appropriate for these situations?

_____

_____

_____

_____

CONTROL CHART

The Control Chart is a special type of line graph you can use to:

  ✎ **Interpret data about a process by creating a picture of the boundaries of acceptable variation**

  ✎ **Objectively determine if a process is *"in control"* or *"out of control"***

Variation is part of everyday life, and no less so in the workplace. For example, there is variation in the length of time it takes to complete a form, variation in the weight and volume of tangible products, and so on.

Regardless of whether you need to track variation in a manufacturing process or a service environment, Control Charts are a useful tool for setting boundaries on the variation within a process. They show you when these boundaries are overstepped, and you can then look for clues to the causes.

Note: There are many types of control charts. This chapter and example cover the P-chart (*i.e., percent defective*) only.

Creating a Control Chart consists of four major steps:

STEP 1: Determine what to measure

STEP 2: Collect the data

STEP 3: Plot the data

STEP 4: Calculate the control limits

Step 1: Determine What To Measure

The first step in constructing a Control Chart is identical to the first step in creating a Run Chart. Identify one key measure you want to track over time or against some base other than time. This measure should be a *"quality/productivity"* (*external customer or internal process*) indicator providing information useful in making decisions.

Possible measures include:

➠ Volume (*i.e., how much over a specified period of time*)

➠ Cycle time (*i.e., how long something takes*)

➠ Errors and defects (*i.e., how many are incorrect over a period of time*)

➠ Waste (*i.e., how much is reworked or rejected*)

The following example illustrates how you can use the Control Chart in a service-related situation.

A major hotel in a large metropolitan area . . .

recently embarked on a quality-improvement effort. Steve, the new Quality Manager, discovered through a customer survey that the billing process was rated *"high"* in importance and received the most complaints. He decided to collect data on the number and types of errors to determine if the billing process was *"in control"* (*i.e., its variation was due to day-to-day or common causes of variation*) and to see where improvements could be made. Steve decided to use a P-chart, which would help him identify the percentage of billing statements that contained errors . . . .

Remarks	Date	# Inspected	Types of Defects				% Defective
			Wrong Room	Wrong Name	Wrong Address	Incomplete Information	
	7-14	50	8	1	1		20
	7-15	50	13			1	28
	7-16	50	11		1		24
	7-17	50	10	3	1	1	30
	7-18	50	12		1	1	28
	7-21	50	14	1			30
	7-22	50	3.5	1	2	1	15
	7-23	50	13	7	2	2	48
	2-24	50	9		1	1	22

(3.5 recorded on 7-22, not a consensus on whether one was a real defect; count .5)

Diagram # 25 - Sample Control Chart data collection sheet

Step 2: Collect The Data

Collect data by using the form provided *(see the Appendix)* or by creating your own, then calculate the percent defective in the space provided. Items to be included on your data collection form include, but are not limited to:

▶ Date

▶ Number inspected

▶ Number defective

▶ Types of defects/errors

▶ Percent defective

Some tips that will help you collect data include:

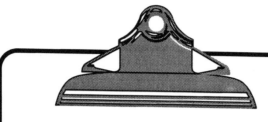

➠ Use a sample containing at least 50 items (the sample should be big enough to give an average of three or more defects per sample)

➠ Avoid taking samples over long periods of time (i.e., try to break large samples up into more manageable two or four-hour time periods versus sampling a full 24-hour day)

➠ Avoid varying sample sizes

➠ Take a minimum of 20 sets of samples

The billing department . . .

had completed basic statistics training, so it wasn't difficult for Steve to find volunteers eager to test their newly acquired skills. Michelle, a billing analyst, offered to inspect 50 hotel bills on a daily basis to find out how many times there were problems with customers' bills *(the number one customer complaint)*. Steve asked her to use the data collection form to keep track of the information that would be used to determine the state of the billing process *(see Diagram # 25)*. . . .

Note: This is a partial chart of the data Michelle collected.

Step 3: Plot The Data

After you've taken at least 20 samples and calculated the percent defective for each, create the plotting scale on the vertical axis of the graph. The scale should reveal whatever is appropriate for your particular measurement. Create a horizontal axis with a point for each sample date.

Plot the individual percent defectives on the graph. Next, compute the average percent defective by adding all of the percent defectives for the individual samples and dividing the result by the total number of samples taken *(in this case 20)*. Draw a horizontal line at the appropriate value, and label it ($\bar{P}=$).

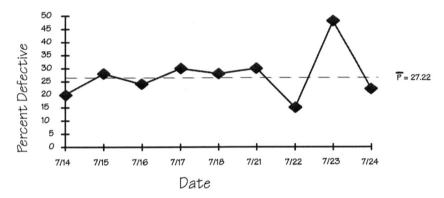

Diagram # 26 - Plot the data

Michelle began the workday . . .

by spending 15 minutes checking the bills for room number errors, as well as address errors, name errors, and incomplete information. She also calculated the percentage of bills that were defective for 20 working days. She then plotted the individual percentages, connected the line, and calculated the average percent defective, or $\bar{P}$ *(see Diagram # 26)*. . . .

Step 4: Calculate The Control Limits

Control limits will tell you if your process is in statistical control *(i.e., the process is exhibiting only common cause variation, or the usual amount of day-to-day variation you might expect from common reasons, such as slightly different materials, methods, machines etc.)*. Think of control limits as invisible boundary lines. As long as the data points are within the boundary lines, everything is "OK." However, when data points are outside the boundary, alarms should go off, and you'll need to investigate why the boundary has been crossed. Control limits are calculated by using the following formula:

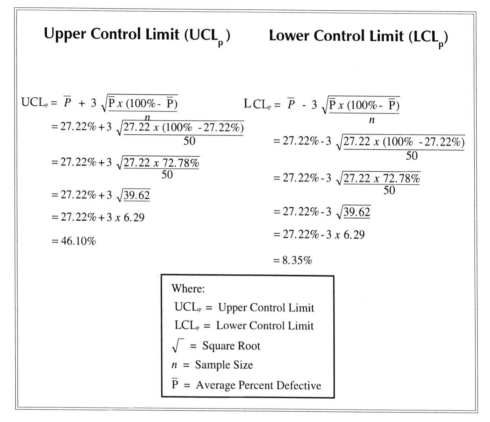

Upper Control Limit (UCL$_p$)   **Lower Control Limit (LCL$_p$)**

$$UCL_p = \overline{P} + 3 \sqrt{\frac{\overline{P} x (100\% - \overline{P})}{n}}$$

$$= 27.22\% + 3 \sqrt{\frac{27.22 \; x \; (100\% - 27.22\%)}{50}}$$

$$= 27.22\% + 3 \sqrt{\frac{27.22 \; x \; 72.78\%}{50}}$$

$$= 27.22\% + 3 \sqrt{39.62}$$

$$= 27.22\% + 3 \; x \; 6.29$$

$$= 46.10\%$$

$$LCL_p = \overline{P} - 3 \sqrt{\frac{\overline{P} x (100\% - \overline{P})}{n}}$$

$$= 27.22\% - 3 \sqrt{\frac{27.22 \; x \; (100\% - 27.22\%)}{50}}$$

$$= 27.22\% - 3 \sqrt{\frac{27.22 \; x \; 72.78\%}{50}}$$

$$= 27.22\% - 3 \sqrt{39.62}$$

$$= 27.22\% - 3 \; x \; 6.29$$

$$= 8.35\%$$

Where:

UCL$_p$ = Upper Control Limit

LCL$_p$ = Lower Control Limit

$\sqrt{}$ = Square Root

n = Sample Size

$\overline{P}$ = Average Percent Defective

Diagram # 27- Calculate control limits

Having plotted all the data points, . . .

Michelle calculated the upper and lower control limits for the billing process (*see Diagram # 27*). She found the corresponding points on the vertical axis of the graph and drew the horizontal lines above and below the average line. She labeled them with the upper and lower control limit values (*see Diagram # 28*). . . .

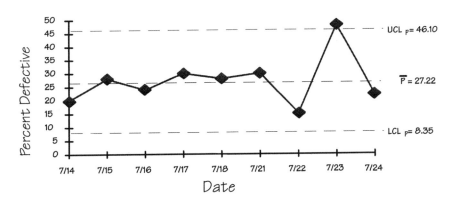

Diagram # 28 - Plot control limits

Follow-up: Decide On Next Steps

What you do next depends upon whether or not your points are within the control limits.

If all points are within the control limits:

➠ Continue with no changes

➠ Recreate the P-chart periodically to double-check process control

➠ Make improvements to the process to reduce common variations

➠ Review to ensure any changes have had a positive effect

If one or more points are outside the control limits:

➠ Investigate and take steps to eliminate the cause(s)

➠ Review to ensure changes have had a positive effect (i.e., uncommon causes have been eliminated)

➠ Take new samples, and create a new P-chart using limits based on the new information

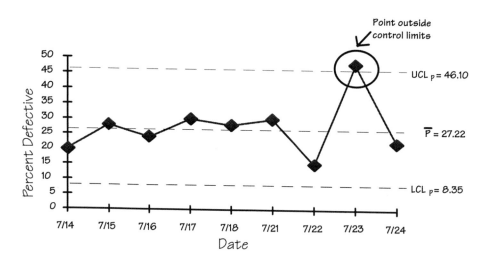

Diagram # 29 - Identify points outside control limits

Having found the billing process to be out of control . . .

(i.e., one or more points outside the control limits; see Diagram # 29), Michelle and two other billing analysts began an investigation into the causes. They knew process improvements could not take place until all special causes, those which caused the data to be outside the control limits, had been identified and eliminated. From recent training, they knew special causes could be assigned to several main categories, including:

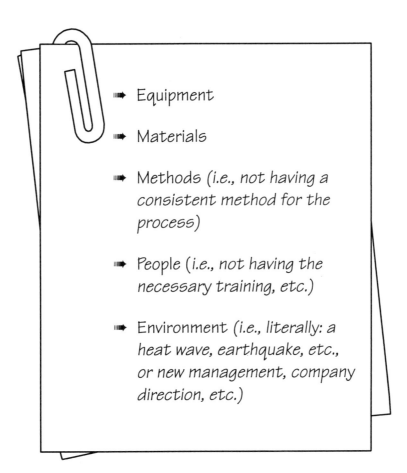

➧ Equipment

➧ Materials

➧ Methods *(i.e., not having a consistent method for the process)*

➧ People *(i.e., not having the necessary training, etc.)*

➧ Environment *(i.e., literally: a heat wave, earthquake, etc., or new management, company direction, etc.)*

They also knew the investigation process wouldn't be easy but were confident real improvements could be made after the process was *"in control."* The next challenge would be reducing the average defect rate substantially, from 27.22% to less than 5%, within six months. With the right problem-solving and quality-improvement tools, they felt they could accomplish their goal.

SUMMARY

In summary, use the Control Chart when:

☑ Trying to determine if a process is in statistical control (*i.e., a process is said to be "out of control" when a data point falls outside of the control limits*).

☑ You want to create a visual representation of process performance. Like the Run Chart, the Control Chart provides a picture of process performance that can be used as a process tracking device.

☑ You want to distinguish between special cause variation (*a clear occurrence of something not normally part of the process*) and common cause variation (*coincidental changes that are inherent in the process*).

☑ You know the process will not change while you are collecting data. The process must not be changed because the intent is to see how the process performs "*naturally.*"

Note: The P-chart was chosen for this guidebook because it has a broad application and is particularly appropriate for service, or non-manufacturing settings. There are many other types of Control Charts. Please look to future resources from the Publications Division of Richard Chang Associates, Inc. for additional Control Chart explanations.

CHAPTER EIGHT WORKSHEET:
CONTROL CHARTS—IDEAS FOR USE

1. What specific opportunities do you have in your organization to use Control Charts?

_____

_____

_____

_____

2. Which of these situations involve a process which you believe to be *"out of control"?* List the specific processes.

_____

_____

_____

_____

_____

_____

_____

3. What will you be measuring in these situations?

_____

_____

_____

HISTOGRAM

A Histogram is a special type of bar chart you can use to:

   🕹 **Communicate information about variation in a process**

   🕹 **Make decisions on the focus of improvement efforts**

The clues given by the Histogram lie in its shape; specifically the height of the bars and patterns of the bars relative to each other.

Creating a Histogram consists of six major steps:

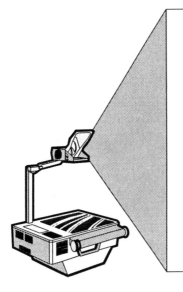

> **STEP 1:** Gather and tabulate the data
>
> **STEP 2:** Calculate the range and interval width
>
> **STEP 3:** Draw the horizontal and vertical axes
>
> **STEP 4:** Tabulate the data by intervals
>
> **STEP 5:** Plot the data
>
> **STEP 6:** Analyze the Histogram

In the ideal process, variation is minimized and under control. This situation is reflected in a Histogram showing a normal, symmetric distribution, or *"bell-shaped"* curve. Most of the measurements fall near the center, with roughly equal numbers falling on either side of the center point *(see Diagram # 30)*.

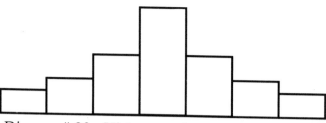

Diagram # 30 - Histogram of a normal distribution

The width of each column represents an interval, or group, of observations within a range, while the height represents the number of observations falling within a given interval.

The example that follows shows how a team used the Histogram to analyze variation in the time it took to process an expense account reimbursement check.

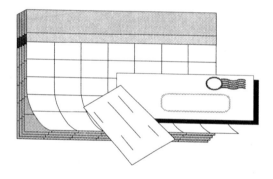

Randy had heard it before. . .

and enough was enough! As one of the analysts in General Accounting, he had heard several complaints about how long it took his department to process an expense reimbursement check. When he looked at the figures for the past few quarters, the records showed the average processing turnaround time varied only slightly from an average of 4.5 days, an acceptable average time. Randy brought the issue up with Danya, the department head. Her response was, "*You're right, the average hasn't changed, but maybe there's something going on that isn't showing up.*" Along with Claire, another analyst in the department, they decided to look closely at the variation. Claire suggested creating a Histogram to compare actual turnaround times. . . .

Step 1: Gather And Tabulate The Data

Histograms are often used to group measures such as time, weight, size, frequency of a certain occurrence, etc., into clusters *(or intervals)* around an average of observations.

The more data used to calculate the average, the more accurate your Histogram will be. Try to get 40 to 50 observations over a predetermined period of time *(a week, a month, etc.)* if you can.

Number of Days Required to Process Each Check (last month)

2.75	3.5	4.25	8	8.25	4
2.5	5.75	2	3	3.25	4.75
3.5	4.5	3.75	7.25	5.25	4.25
2.25	1.5	7.25	3.75	4.25	5.5
6	4.5	8	4.75	5	2
6.25	4	8.5	4.25	2.5	4.75
3.25	4.5	1.75	6.5	3.25	4.25

Diagram # 31 - Tabulated data for Histogram

Randy and Claire reviewed the data . . .

for the last month and discovered 42 expense reimbursement checks had been processed. The average turnaround time was exactly what it was for the quarter—4.5 days. They transferred the data from the department's files to a data sheet in order to have all of the numbers in one place *(see Diagram # 31). . . .*

Step 2: Calculate The Range And Interval Width

Before you begin to plot the data, set up a scale and decide on the intervals for the data.

➠ **Calculate the range:**
Simply calculate the difference between the lowest and highest numbers in the data collected (*e.g. if the highest number in the data is 22.6 inches and the lowest is 12.2 inches, the range would be 10.4 inches*).

➠ **Calculate the interval width:**
Decide how many bars you want to show on the Histogram. The more bars you have, the narrower each bar (*or interval*) will be, and vice versa. Usually six to twelve work best. To determine the width of an interval, divide the range by the number of bars. Each interval represents a bar on the Histogram. In the above example, the interval width would be 1.3 inches if you were going to use eight bars (*10.4 inches divided by 8*), or 1.04 inches if you were going to use 10 bars (*10.4 divided by 10*).

Range = 8.5 - 1.5 = 7 days
Interval width = .7 days (*7 days ÷ 10 bars*)

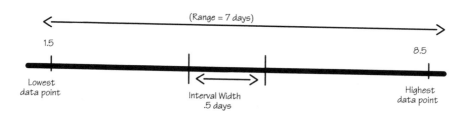

Diagram # 32 - Calculating the range and interval width

> ## *Claire and Randy calculated the range . . .*
> of data from the table. They decided to use a seven-day period. They
> thought about using only seven bars for the Histogram, equaling an interval
> width of one day, but decided to use 10, giving them a width of .7 days *(see
> Diagram # 32)*. Claire felt the additional breakdown of data would give them
> a clearer picture of the situation. . . .

Step 3: Draw The Horizontal And Vertical Axes

Draw the horizontal axis. Plot intervals on this axis using previously calculated interval widths.

Draw the vertical axis. Select the highest point for the axis by dividing the number of observations by three and use the resulting number *(i.e., if you had 60 observations, your scale for the vertical axis would go up to 20)*.

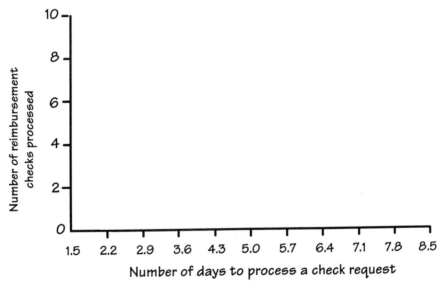

Diagram # 33 - Draw the horizontal and vertical axes

> ## *To simplify things, . . .*
> Randy first set the scale for the vertical axis at 14 *(42 divided by three)*. He
> looked at the table of data and realized none of the numbers ever came close
> to showing up 14 times, so he lowered the scale to ten. *"That should do it,"* he
> thought as he finished drawing the two axes on the graph paper. . . .

Step 4: Tabulate The Data By Intervals

To plot the bars on a Histogram, organize observations and group them into intervals.

Interval	Number of Observations
1.5 - 2.2	IIII
2.2 - 2.9	IIII
2.9 - 3.6	IIIHI
3.6 - 4.3	IIIHIIIII
4.3 - 5.0	IIIHII
5.0 - 5.7	III
5.7 - 6.4	III
6.4 - 7.1	I
7.1 - 7.8	II
7.8 - 8.5	IIII

Diagram # 34 - Tabulating the data by intervals

"Setting up the table . . .

to organize the data by intervals was a breeze," thought Randy. Claire called out the numbers from the original data table and he made tick marks in the new table. *"Now, all we need to do is draw the bars on the Histogram to these heights and we'll be finished,"* said Randy as Claire called out the last number *(see Diagram # 34)*. . . .

Step 5: Plot The Data

Once the intervals are determined and the data categorized according to how many of the measurements fall within each interval, the next step is to plot the data on the Histogram.

Simply draw the bars for each interval. The height of each bar represents the number of measures corresponding to its interval on the horizontal axis.

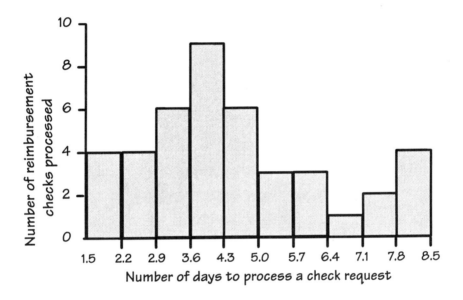

Diagram # 35 - Drawing the bars

With pencil in hand, . . .

Danya began drawing bars on the Histogram, beginning with the four observations for the first interval of 1.5 to 2.2 and continuing to the four observations for the last interval of 7.8 to 8.5. *"The shape of our Histogram doesn't look right,"* said Danya, *"the data should be grouped tightly around the center, shouldn't it?" (see Diagram # 35)*. . . .

Step 6: Analyze the Histogram

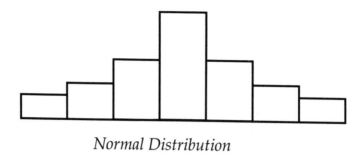

Normal Distribution

Analyze the Histogram to find out what is happening in your process. The example above illustrates normal distribution. Most of the measurements are concentrated in the middle intervals, indicating variation from the average is under control and manageable.

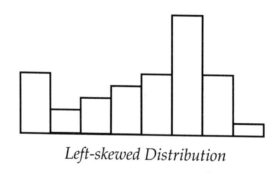

Left-skewed Distribution

The second Histogram shows a process which is skewed to the left. This indicates something is happening in the process to produce a group of measures on the far left of the scale. This is caused by inconsistencies in the process, such as a new employee taking longer to complete a task *(if completion time is the measure)*, inconsistent procedures, and so on.

When your Histogram shows a left or right skew, track the data points on the skewed end to find what the common patterns *(or potential causes)* are.

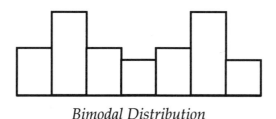

Bimodal Distribution

The third Histogram illustrates a process with clusters of measures on opposite ends of the scale *(bimodal distribution).* This indicates serious inconsistencies in a process. Using the average to measure the performance of the process is virtually meaningless, since most of the measurements occur well above or below the average.

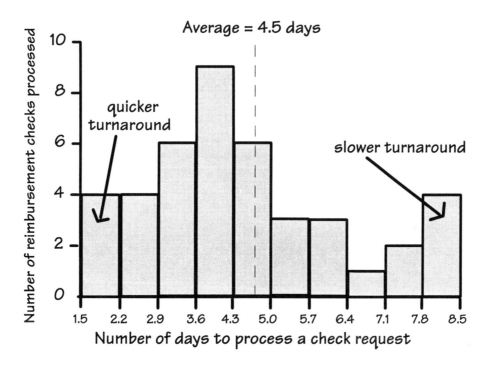

Diagram # 36 - Analyzing the Histogram

The Histogram . . .

showed an interesting pattern *(see Diagram # 36)*. The average time had already been calculated as 4.5 days *(the total of the times divided by 42 observations for the month)*. The Histogram showed the largest grouping in the interval of 3.6 to 4.3 days, which was close to the average, and made sense.

"But why are the bars getting higher for the last two intervals, between 7.1 days and 8.5 days?" asked Claire. *"If it wasn't for those intervals, our average would be lower. Why do some checks take that long to process anyway?"*

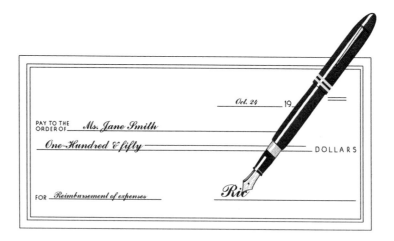

"I think I know what is going on here," replied Danya. *"The Histogram should be tapering off on the left side too, but it doesn't. 'Rush' requests from senior managers account for the requests being turned around in a day or two. That explains the relatively high number in the interval of 1.5 to 2.2 days. When we deal with those special cases we have to set aside someone else's request, holding it up for a couple of days—and they show up on the right side of the Histogram."*

"So we may be receiving complaints about slow turnaround because of the special treatment we give to the checks for senior managers, right?" asked Randy.

Follow-Up: Decide On Next Steps

After you have analyzed your Histogram, you might find yourself in one of the following situations:

➠ Your analysis has produced useful answers. You've learned what is happening in your process, and why the variation occurs in a certain way *(e.g., a skewed, bimodal, or other abnormal distribution shows up in your Histogram)*. As a result, you need to reduce the variation to a target level and decide when to plot the next Histogram *(to track progress)*.

➠ The Histogram's shape provided clues about the type of variation occurring. It is skewed to the right, meaning the variation is occurring mainly on that end of your measurement scale. You have an idea about what's behind the picture but can't put your finger on the precise underlying cause. In this case, you need to dig deeper to find out what is really going on.

Note: Appropriate tools for further analysis might include Run Charts, Control Charts, and other tools explained in this guidebook.

➠ You are not sure what the clues are behind the Histogram's shape. In this case, it is a good idea to bring others into the picture. Ask for their help in analyzing why the data is skewed, bimodal, or any other abnormal shape.

Note: Appropriate tools for further analysis might include Brainstorming, Cause and Effect Diagrams, and other tools explained in *Continuous Improvement Tools Volume 1*.

In summary, use a Histogram when:

☑ You want to verify or investigate whether a problem really exists. The Histogram serves as an indicator of a problem, and further investigation can verify the source or cause of the problem.

☑ You want a tool to communicate distribution of data, or to create a *"picture"* of variation within a process. Using a Histogram when working together as a group is a very effective way of ensuring a common understanding of the information.

☑ You want to track changes in process variation across time *(e.g., by using your initial Histogram as a base line, and creating new ones to measure changes as you improve the underlying process).*

CHAPTER NINE WORKSHEET:
HISTOGRAMS—IDEAS FOR USE

1. What specific opportunities do you have in your organization to use Histograms?

_____

_____

_____

2. What types of data and measures are needed to create these Histograms?

_____

_____

3. How many observations will you gather?

_____

_____

4. What tools are appropriate to further analyze the situation, if necessary?

_____

_____

_____

CHAPTER TEN

SUMMARY

Improving the quality of your organization's products and services can seem both an elusive goal and a challenging task. But why should it seem elusive? You may have found, as many organizations have, the concept of quality often means different things to different people. Unless the concept, or goal, is clearly defined and understood by all team members, people will use their own path to reach their individual definition of quality improvement.

This guidebook provides several tools to help your organization find common approaches to quality-improvement efforts so that your whole team can move forward in unison toward common goals.

The true challenge of organizational improvement efforts lies in the many *"How?"* questions you need to ask at the outset *(e.g., How do we track our quality-improvement efforts? How do we measure quality?)*

Armed with the tools, ideas, and examples in this book and in *Continuous Improvement Tools Volume 1*, you can easily answer such *"How?"* questions. Just think, you're already halfway to achieving your goals!

With a unified team, a clear goal, and proven tools, you're all set to build real improvements and real quality into your organization.

WORKSHEETS AND REPRODUCIBLE FORMS

The pages in the Appendix are provided for you to photocopy and use appropriately.

TREE DIAGRAM WORKSHEET

Answer the following questions when preparing for a Tree Diagram session:

1. Describe the goal of the Tree Diagram session (*i.e., the corrective action to be implemented*):

_____

_____

_____

_____

2. What are the major subgoals (*i.e., major things that need to be done in order to get to the main goal*)?

_____

_____

_____

3. What are the first tasks that need to be done to implement the corrective action?

_____

_____

_____

_____

4. Who else should review the Tree Diagram after it is finished?

_____

_____

_____

_____

_____

_____

_____

_____

_____

5. What is your next step after completing the Tree Diagram?

_____

_____

_____

_____

_____

_____

_____

_____

TREE DIAGRAM

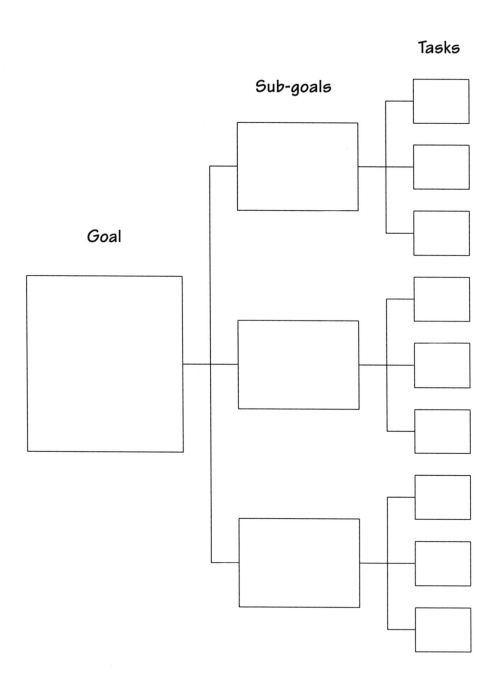

PARETO CHART WORKSHEET

Answer the following questions when creating and analyzing your Pareto Chart:

1. List the different categories of problems or causes:

_____

_____

_____

_____

2. What is the most frequently occurring problem?

_____

_____

_____

_____

3. What is the most important problem to the customer?

_____

_____

_____

_____

4. What is the cost of correcting the problem?

_____

_____

_____

_____

_____

_____

_____

5. What is the cost of not correcting the problem?

_____

_____

_____

_____

_____

_____

_____

PARETO CHART

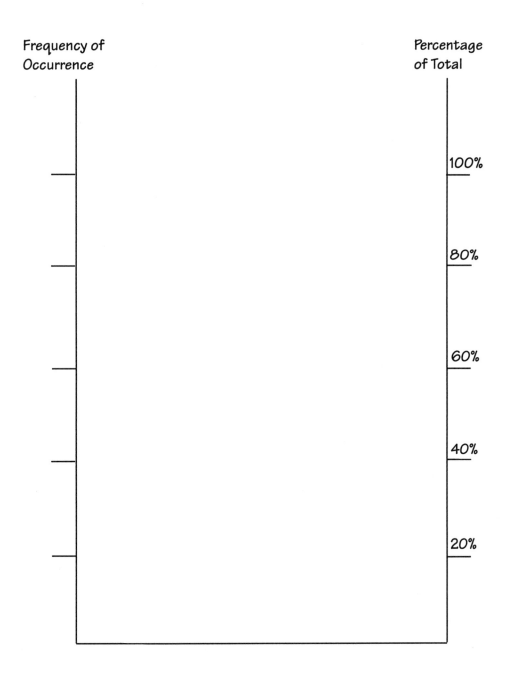

Frequency of
Occurrence

Percentage
of Total

100%

80%

60%

40%

20%

SEQUENCE FLOW CHART
WORKSHEET

Answer the following questions when preparing for a Sequence
Flow Chart session:

1. Who owns the process you are analyzing?

_____

_____

_____

_____

_____

2. What are the boundaries of the process you are analyzing (*i.e.,*
where the process starts and ends)?

Starting point:

_____

_____

Ending point:

_____

_____

3. What do you hope to achieve by analyzing this process?

_____

_____

_____

_____

_____

_____

_____

4. What is at least one area of measurement for the process you
are analyzing ? *(This question may be answered after you have
completed the flowchart.)*

_____

_____

_____

_____

5. How will you know if the process is improved?

_____

_____

_____

_____

_____

SEQUENCE FLOW CHART

WHO / TASK										Time-Per-Task	Elasped Time
TOTAL											

PROCESS FLOW CHART
WORKSHEET

Answer the following questions when preparing for a Process Flow Chart session:

1. Who owns the process you are analyzing?

_____

_____

_____

_____

2. What are the boundaries of the process you are analyzing *(i.e., where the process starts and ends)?*

_____

_____

_____

_____

_____

3. What do you hope to achieve by analyzing this process?

_____

_____

_____

_____

_____

_____

_____

_____

4. What is at least one area of measurement for the process you are analyzing? (*This question may be answered after you have completed the flow chart.*)

_____

_____

_____

_____

_____

_____

5. How will you know if the process is improved?

_____

_____

_____

_____

SCATTER DIAGRAM WORKSHEET

Answer the following questions prior to completing the Scatter Diagram:

1. What two variables are being compared?

_____

_____

_____

_____

_____

2. Why are you creating a Scatter Diagram?

_____

_____

_____

_____

3. How will the information be used?

_____

_____

_____

_____

4. What additional measurements may need to be taken? *(This question may be answered after you have completed the Scatter Diagram.)*

_____

_____

_____

_____

_____

_____

_____

5. What are your planned next steps?

_____

_____

_____

_____

_____

_____

_____

RUN CHART WORKSHEET

Answer the following questions prior to completing the Run Chart:

1. Why are you creating a Run Chart?

_____

_____

_____

_____

_____

2. What are you measuring?

_____

_____

_____

_____

_____

3. How will the information be used?

_____

_____

_____

4. What additional measurements may need to be taken? *(This question may be answered after you have completed the Run Chart.)*

_____

_____

_____

_____

_____

_____

_____

5. What are your planned next steps?

_____

_____

_____

_____

_____

_____

_____

_____

_____

_____

CONTROL CHART WORKSHEET

Answer the following questions prior to completing the Control Chart:

1. Is a P-chart appropriate for this situation?

_____

_____

_____

_____

_____

2. What are you measuring?

_____

_____

_____

_____

_____

3. How will the information be used?

_____

_____

_____

_____

_____

_____

4. What additional measurements may need to be taken? *(This question may be answered after you have completed the Control Chart.)*

_____

_____

_____

_____

_____

_____

_____

_____

5. What are your planned next steps?

_____

_____

_____

_____

DATA COLLECTION SHEET

Remarks	Date	# Inspected	Types of Defects				% Defective

HISTOGRAM WORKSHEET

1. What is the goal of creating the Histogram?

_____

_____

_____

_____

2. What data will you use for the Histogram?

_____

_____

_____

_____

_____

3. What interval width will you use? (_How many bars do you want to display?_)

_____

_____

_____

_____

4. Who needs to review the Histogram after it is created? Why?

_____

_____

_____

_____

_____

_____

_____

5. What are the necessary next steps after the Histogram is created and analyzed?

_____

_____

_____

_____

_____

_____

_____

_____

_____

THE PRACTICAL GUIDEBOOK COLLECTION
FROM RICHARD CHANG ASSOCIATES, INC.
PUBLICATIONS DIVISION

Our Practical Guidebook Collection is growing to meet the challenges of the ever-changing workplace of the 90's. Look for these and other titles from Richard Chang Associates, Inc. on your bookstore shelves and in book catalogs.

QUALITY IMPROVEMENT SERIES

- Meetings That Work!
- Continuous Improvement Tools Volume 1
- Continuous Improvement Tools Volume 2
- Step-By-Step Problem Solving
- Satisfying Internal Customers First!
- Continuous Process Improvement
- Improving Through Benchmarking
- Succeeding As A Self-Managed Team
- Reengineering In Action

MANAGEMENT SKILLS SERIES

- Coaching Through Effective Feedback
- Expanding Leadership Impact
- Mastering Change Management
- On-The-Job Orientation And Training
- Re-Creating Teams During Transitions

HIGH PERFORMANCE TEAM SERIES

- Success Through Teamwork
- Team Decision-Making Techniques
- Measuring Team Performance
- Building A Dynamic Team

HIGH-IMPACT TRAINING SERIES

- Creating High-Impact Training
- Identifying Targeted Training Needs
- Applying Successful Training Techniques
- Measuring The Impact Of Training
- Make Your Training Results Last

ADDITIONAL RESOURCES
FROM RICHARD CHANG ASSOCIATES, INC.

Improve your training sessions and seminars with the ideal tools—videos from Richard Chang Associates, Inc. You and your team will easily relate to the portrayals of real-life workplace situations. You can apply our innovative techniques to your own situations for immediate results.

TRAINING VIDEOTAPES

Mastering Change Management*
Turning Obstacles Into Opportunities

Step-By-Step Problem Solving*
A Practical Approach To Solving Problems On The Job

Quality: You Don't Have To Be Sick To Get Better**
Individuals Do Make a Difference

Achieving Results Through Quality Improvement**

*Authored by Dr. Richard Chang and produced by Double Vision Studios.
**Produced by American Media Inc. in conjunction with Richard Chang Associates, Inc.
  Each video includes a Facilitator's Guide.

"THE HUMAN EDGE SERIES" VIDEOTAPES

Total Quality: Myths, Methods, Or Miracles
Featuring Drs. Ken Blanchard and Richard Chang

Empowering The Quality Effort
Featuring Drs. Ken Blanchard and Richard Chang

Produced by Double Vision Studios.

"THE TOTAL QUALITY SERIES"
TRAINING VIDEOTAPES AND WORKBOOKS

Building Commitment *(Telly Award Winner)*
How To Build Greater Commitment To Your TQ Efforts

Teaming Up
How To Successfully Participate On Quality-Improvement Teams

Applied Problem Solving
How To Solve Problems As An Individual Or On A Team

Self-Directed Evaluation
How To Establish Feedback Methods To Self-Monitor Improvements

Authored by Dr. Richard Chang and produced by Double Vision Studios, each videotape from *"The Total Quality Series"* includes a *Facilitator's Guide* and five *Participant Workbooks* with each purchase. Additional *Participant Workbooks* are available for purchase.

EVALUATION AND FEEDBACK FORM

We need your help to continuously improve the quality of the resources provided through the Richard Chang Associates, Inc., Publications Division. We would greatly appreciate your input and suggestions regarding this particular guidebook, as well as future guidebook interests.

Please photocopy this form before completing it, since other readers may use this guidebook. Thank you in advance for your feedback.

Guidebook Title: _____

1. Overall, how would you rate your *level of satisfaction* with this guidebook? Please circle your response.

    Extremely Dissatisfied   Satisfied   Extremely Satisfied

         1   2   3   4   5

2. What specific *concepts or methods* did you find <u>most</u> helpful?

    _____

    _____

3. What specific *concepts or methods* did you find <u>least</u> helpful?

    _____

    _____

4. As an individual who may purchase additional guidebooks in the future, what *characteristics/features/benefits* are most important to you in making a decision to purchase a guidebook (*or another similar book*)?

    _____

    _____

5. What additional *subject matter/topic areas* would you like to see addressed in future guidebooks?

    _____

    _____

Name (*optional*): _____

Address: _____

C/S/Z: _____   **Phone (   )** _____